P9-CMR-436

Middle
Ages
Primary Sources

Middle Ages
Ages
Primary Sources

JUDSON KNIGHT
Edited by Judy Galens

AN IMPRINT OF THE GALE GROUP

DETROIT · NEW YORK · SAN FRANCISCO
LONDON · BOSTON · WOODBRIDGE, CT

Middle Ages: Primary Sources

Judson Knight

Judy Galens, *Editor*

Staff

Diane Sawinski, *U•X•L Senior Editor*
Carol DeKane Nagel, *U•X•L Managing Editor*
Thomas L. Romig, *U•X•L Publisher*

Margaret Chamberlain, *Permissions Associate (Pictures)*
Maria Franklin, *Permissions Manager*

Randy Bassett, *Imaging Database Supervisor*
Daniel Newell, *Imaging Specialist*
Pamela A. Reed, *Image Coordinator*
Robyn V. Young, *Senior Image Editor*

Rita Wimberley, *Senior Buyer*
Evi Seoud, *Assistant Production Manager*
Dorothy Maki, *Manufacturing Manager*

Pamela A. E. Galbreath, *Senior Art Director*
Kenn Zorn, *Product Design Manager*

Marco Di Vita, the Graphix Group, *Typesetting*

Cover photograph of Augustine reproduced courtesy of the Library of Congress.

Library of Congress Cataloging-in-Publication Data

Knight, Judson
    Middle ages. Primary sources / [compiled by] Judson Knight ;
Judy Galens, editor.
      p. cm.
    Includes bibliographical references and index.
    ISBN 0-7876-4860-4
      1. Middle Ages—History—Sources. I. Knight, Judson. II. Galens, Judy,
  1968-
  D113.M49 2000 v.4
  909.07–dc21

                                        00-059441
                                           CIP

Contents

Reader's Guide

The Middle Ages was an era of great changes in civilization, a transition between ancient times and the modern world. Lasting roughly from A.D. 500 to 1500, the period saw the growth of the Roman Catholic Church in Western Europe and the spread of the Islamic faith in the Middle East. Around the world, empires—the Byzantine, Mongol, and Incan—rose and fell, and the first nation-states emerged in France, England, and Spain. Despite the beauty of illuminated manuscripts, soaring Gothic cathedrals, and the literary classics of Augustine and Dante, Europe's civilization lagged far behind that of the technologically advanced, administratively organized, and economically wealthy realms of the Arab world, West Africa, India, and China.

Middle Ages: Primary Sources offers nineteen full or excerpted documents written during the Middle Ages. Covering such topics as cultures in conflict; personal life; the relationship between the church and government; and the writing of history and fiction, the documents give a rich sense of life in the Middle Ages, as told by its participants. Entries include Marco Polo's description of his travels in China; an excerpt from *The Thousand and One Nights*, better known in the West as *Arabian Nights;* and Japan's "Seventeen-Article Constitution," written by Prince Shotoku Taishi.

Format

Each of the four chapters of *Middle Ages: Primary Sources* begins with a historical overview, followed by several full or excerpted documents.

Each primary source document is accompanied by several sections of supporting information:

- **Introductory material** places the document and its author in a historical context
- **Things to remember** offers readers important background information about the featured text
- **What happened next** discusses the impact of the document on both the author and his or her audience
- **Did you know** provides interesting facts about each document and its author
- **For more information** presents sources for further reading on the authors and the documents

Additional features

Over thirty illustrations and several sidebar boxes exploring high-interest people and topics bring the text to life. Each excerpt is accompanied by a glossary running alongside the primary document that defines terms and ideas discussed within the document. The volume also contains a timeline of events, a general glossary, and an index offering easy access to the people, places, and subjects discussed throughout *Middle Ages: Primary Sources*.

Dedication

To Margaret, my mother; to Deidre, my wife; and to Tyler, my daughter.

Comments and suggestions

We welcome your comments on this work as well as your suggestions for topics to be featured in future editions of *Middle Ages: Primary Sources*. Please write: Editors, *Middle Ages: Primary Sources*, U•X•L, 27500 Drake Rd., Farmington Hills, MI 48331-3535; call toll-free: 1-800-877-4253; fax: 248-699-8097; or send e-mail via www.galegroup.com.

Timeline of Events
in the Middle Ages

135   Banished from Jerusalem by the Romans, Jews begin to spread throughout the Mediterranean region.

184   The Revolt of the Yellow Turbans, which will be suppressed five years later by General Ts'ao Ts'ao, signals the beginning of the end for China's Han dynasty.

220   The Han dynasty of China comes to an end, plunging the country into three centuries of turmoil. This begins with the period of the Three Kingdoms from 220 to 265. More than a thousand years later, **Lo Kuanchung** will retell the story of this era in *Romance of the Three Kingdoms*.

300s   Buddhism, which originated in India, begins to take hold in China.

312   Roman emperor Constantine converts to Christianity. As a result, the empire that once persecuted Christians will embrace their religion and eventually will begin to persecute other religions.

410	Led by Alaric, the Visigoths sack Rome, dealing the Western Roman Empire a blow from which it will never recover.
413–425	Deeply affected—as are most Roman citizens—by the Visigoths' attack on Rome, **Augustine** writes *City of God,* one of the most important books of the Middle Ages.
Mid-400s	Angles, Saxons, and Jutes from Scandinavia invade the former Roman colony of Britain.
451	Roman troops score their last important victory, against Attila's Huns in Gaul.
452	Leo I, the first significant bishop of Rome (in other words, pope), persuades Attila not to attack Rome itself: an early sign of the political authority that will be wielded by the church during the Middle Ages.
455	The Vandals sack Rome.
476	The German leader Odoacer removes Emperor Romulus Augustulus and crowns himself "king of Italy." This incident marks the end of the Western Roman Empire.
481	The Merovingian Age, named for the only powerful dynasty in Western Europe during the period, begins when Clovis takes the throne in France.
496	Clovis converts to Christianity, an action later documented by the historian **Gregory of Tours** in his *History of the Franks*. By establishing strong ties with the pope, Clovis forges a strong church-state relationship that will continue throughout the medieval period.
500	Date commonly cited as beginning of Middle Ages.
500–1000	Era in European history often referred to as the Dark Ages, or Early Middle Ages.
532	Thanks in large part to the counsel of his wife Theodora, Justinian—greatest of Byzantine emperors—takes a strong stand in the Nika Revolt, ensuring his continued power.
534–563	Belisarius and other generals under orders from Justinian recapture much of the Western Roman Empire, including parts of Italy, Spain, and North Africa. The

victories are costly, however, and soon after Justinian's death these lands will fall back into the hands of barbarian tribes such as the Vandals and Lombards.

535   Justinian establishes his legal code, a model for the laws in many Western nations today.

552   A collection of scriptures, sent as a gift from the court of the Paekche kingdom in Korea to Japan, helps introduce Buddhism to Japan.

c. 565   Greek historian **Procopius** dies. Procopius's scandalous and gossipy account of the rule of Justinian, *Secret History,* is not published until many centuries later.

589   More than three centuries of upheaval in China come to an end with the establishment of the Sui dynasty.

590   Pope Gregory I begins his fourteen-year reign. Also known as Gregory the Great, he ensures the survival of the church and becomes one of its greatest medieval leaders.

604   Prince **Shotoku Taishi** of Japan issues his "Seventeen-Article Constitution."

618   A revolt agasint the cruel Sui dynasty leads to the establishment of the highly powerful and efficient T'ang dynasty in China.

622   Muhammad and his followers escape the city of Mecca. This event, known as the *hegira,* marks the beginning of the Muslim calendar.

632–661   Following the death of Muhammad, the Arab Muslims are led by a series of four caliphs who greatly expand Muslim territories to include most of the Middle East.

661   The fifth caliph, Mu'awiya, founds the Umayyad caliphate, which will rule the Muslim world from Damascus, Syria, until 750.

732   A force led by Charles Martel repels Moorish invaders at Tours, halting Islam's advance into Western Europe.

750   A descendant of Muhammad's uncle Abbas begins killing off all the Umayyad leaders and establishes the Abbasid caliphate in Baghdad, Iraq.

751	The Carolingian Age begins when Charles Martel's son Pepin III, with the support of the pope, removes the last Merovingian king from power.
751	Defeated by Arab armies at Talas, China's T'ang dynasty begins to decline. A revolt led by An Lu-shan in 755 adds to its troubles.
768	Reign of Charlemagne, greatest ruler of Western Europe during the Early Middle Ages, begins.
793	Viking raiders destroy the church at Lindisfarne off the coast of England. Lindisfarne was one of the places where civilized learning had weathered the darkest years of the Middle Ages. Thus begins two centuries of terror as more invaders pour out of Scandinavia and spread throughout Europe.
800s	Feudalism takes shape in Western Europe.
800	Pope Leo III crowns Charlemagne "Emperor of All the Romans." This marks the beginning of the political alliance later to take shape under Otto the Great as the Holy Roman Empire.
820	A group of Vikings settles in northwestern France, where they will become known as Normans.
900s	The 264 stories that make up *The Thousand and One Nights,* a collection of tales from Indian, Persian, and Arab sources, are first assembled.
907	China's T'ang dynasty comes to an end after almost three centuries of rule, and the empire enters a period of instability known as "Five Dynasties and Ten Kingdoms."
960	Beginning of the Sung dynasty in China.
962	Having conquered most of Central Europe, Otto the Great is crowned emperor in Rome, reviving Charlemagne's title. From this point on, most German kings are also crowned ruler of the Holy Roman Empire.
987	The last Carolingian ruler of France dies without an heir, and Hugh Capet takes the throne, establishing a dynasty that will last until 1328.
1000–1300	Era in European history often referred to as the High Middle Ages.

1000s Guilds, which had existed in ancient times but disappeared from Western Europe during the Early Middle Ages, come back into existence.

1002 In Japan, Murasaki Shikibu begins writing the *Tale of Genji,* the world's first novel. This romantic tale heavily influences another Japanese woman writer, **Lady Sarashina,** who reflects that influence in her autobiography, *The Diary of Lady Sarashina.*

1002 Ethelred the Unready of England marries Emma of Normandy, giving the Normans a foothold in Britain.

1025 Emperor Basil II dies, having taken the Byzantine Empire to its greatest height since Justinian five centuries earlier; however, it begins a rapid decline soon afterward.

1042 Edward the Confessor, son of Ethelred the Unready and Emma of Normandy, becomes English king. During his reign many Normans settle in England.

1054 After centuries of disagreement over numerous issues, the Greek Orthodox Church and the Roman Catholic Church officially separate.

1060 Five years after Turks seize control of Baghdad from the declining Abbasid caliphate, their leader, Toghril Beg, declares himself sultan and thus establishes the Seljuk dynasty.

1066 William the Conqueror leads an invading force that defeats an Anglo-Saxon army at Hastings and wins control of England. The Norman invasion, which has its roots in King Ethelred's marriage to Emma of Normandy in 1002, is the most important event of medieval English history, greatly affecting the future of English culture and language. This event will be documented later by historian **William of Malmesbury** in his work *Gesta regum Anglorum.*

c. 1067 **Al-Bekri**, a Spanish Muslim, travels to the great empire of Ghana in West Africa, a trip he will later write about in *Al-Masalik wa 'l-Mamalik.*

1071 The Seljuk Turks defeat Byzantine forces at the Battle of Manzikert in Armenia. As a result, the Turks gain a foothold in Asia Minor (today known as Turkey) and the Byzantine Empire begins a long, slow decline.

1075–77 Pope **Gregory VII** and Holy Roman Emperor **Henry IV** become embroiled in a church-state struggle called the Investiture Controversy, a debate over whether popes or emperors should have the right to appoint local bishops. Deserted by his supporters, Henry stands barefoot in the snow for three days outside the gates of a castle in Canossa, Italy, waiting to beg the pope's forgiveness.

1080 Invaders from Morocco destroy Ghana, the first significant kingdom in sub-Saharan Africa.

1084 Reversing the results of an earlier round in the Investiture Controversy, **Henry IV** takes Rome and forcibly removes **Gregory VII** from power. The pope dies soon afterward, broken and humiliated.

1084 Ssu-ma Kuang, an official in the Sung dynasty, completes his monumental history of China, *Comprehensive Mirror for Aid in Government*.

1092 Following the death of their sultan Malik Shah, the Seljuk Turks begin to decline.

1094 Norman warrior Bohemond, son of Robert Guiscard, takes control of Rome from **Henry IV** and hands the city over to Pope Urban II. Fearing the Normans' power and aware that he owes them a great debt, Urban looks for something to divert their attention.

1095 Byzantine Emperor Alexis Comnenus asks Urban II for military assistance against the Turks. Urban preaches a sermon to raise support at the Council of Clermont in France, and in the resulting fervor the First Crusade begins. Among its leaders are Bohemond and his nephew Tancred.

1096–97 A pathetic sideshow called the Peasants' Crusade plays out before the real First Crusade gets underway. The peasants begin by robbing and killing thousands of Jews in Germany; then, led by Peter the Hermit, they march toward the Holy Land, wreaking havoc as they go. In Anatolia a local Turkish sultan leads them into a trap, and most of the peasants are killed.

1099 The First Crusade ends in victory for the Europeans as they conquer Jerusalem. It is a costly victory, however—one in which thousands of innocent Muslims, as well as many Europeans, have been brutally slaughtered—and it sows resentment between Muslims and Christians that remains strong today.

c. 1100–1300 Many of the aspects of life most commonly associated with the Middle Ages, including heraldry and chivalry, make their appearance in Western Europe during this period. Returning crusaders adapt the defensive architecture they observed in fortresses of the Holy Land, resulting in the familiar design of the medieval castle. This is also the era of romantic and heroic tales such as those of King Arthur.

1118 After being banished because of her part in a conspiracy against her brother, the Byzantine emperor, **Anna Comnena** begins writing the *Alexiad,* a history of Byzantium in the period 1069–1118.

1147–49 In the disastrous Second Crusade, armies from Europe are double-crossed by their crusader allies in the Latin Kingdom of Jerusalem. They fail to recapture Edessa and suffer a heavy defeat at Damascus.

1159 Holy Roman Emperor Frederick I Barbarossa begins a quarter-century of fruitless, costly wars in which the Ghibellines and Guelphs—factions representing pro-imperial and pro-church forces, respectively—fight for control of northern Italy.

1165 A letter supposedly written by Prester John, a Christian monarch in the East, appears in Europe. Over the centuries that follow, Europeans will search in vain for Prester John, hoping for his aid in their war against Muslim forces.

c. 1175 **Usamah ibn Munqidh** writes his *Memoirs,* describing from a Muslim point of view the uneasy relationship between the Arabs of the Middle East and the Christian Europeans who occupied their lands as a result of the Crusades.

1182 France under Philip II Augustus becomes the first European country to expel all its Jews.

1187 Muslim armies under Saladin deal the crusaders a devastating blow at the Battle of Hittin in Palestine. Shortly afterward Saladin leads his armies in the reconquest of Jerusalem.

1189 In response to Saladin's victories, Europeans launch the Third Crusade.

1191 Led by Richard I of England and Philip II of France, crusaders take the city of Acre in Palestine.

1192 Richard I signs a treaty with Saladin, ending the Third Crusade.

1198 Pope Innocent III begins an eighteen-year reign that marks the high point of the church's power. Despite his great influence, however, when he calls for a new crusade to the Holy Land, he gets little response—a sign that the spirit behind the Crusades is dying.

1202 Four years after the initial plea from the pope, the Fourth Crusade begins. Instead of going to the Holy Land, however, the crusaders become involved in a power struggle for the Byzantine throne.

1204 Acting on orders from the powerful city-state of Venice, crusaders take Constantinople, forcing the Byzantines to retreat to Trebizond in Turkey. The Fourth Crusade ends with the establishment of the Latin Empire.

1206 Genghis Khan unites the Mongols for the first time in their history and soon afterward leads them to war against the Sung dynasty in China.

1208 Pope Innocent III launches the Albigensian Crusade against the Cathars, a heretical sect in southern France.

1215 English noblemen force King John to sign the Magna Carta, which grants much greater power to the nobility. Ultimately the agreement will lead to increased freedom for the people from the power of both king and nobles.

1217–21 In the Fifth Crusade, armies from England, Germany, Hungary, and Austria attempt unsuccessfully to conquer Egypt.

1227 Genghis Khan dies, having conquered much of China and Central Asia, thus laying the foundation for the largest empire in history.

1228–29 The Sixth Crusade, led by Holy Roman Emperor Frederick II, results in a treaty that briefly restores Christian control of Jerusalem—and does so with a minimum of bloodshed.

1229 The brutal Albigensian Crusade ends. Not only are the Cathars destroyed, but so is much of the French nobility, thus greatly strengthening the power of the French king.

1231 Pope Gregory IX establishes the Inquisition, a court through which the church will investigate, try, and punish cases of heresy.

c. 1235 The empire of Mali, most powerful realm in sub-Saharan Africa at the time, takes shape under the leadership of Sundiata Keita.

1239–40 In the Seventh Crusade, Europeans make another failed attempt to retake the Holy Land.

1241 After six years of campaigns in which they sliced across Russia and Eastern Europe, a Mongol force is poised to take Vienna, Austria, and thus to swarm into Western Europe. But when their leader, Batu Khan, learns that the Great Khan Ogodai is dead, he rushes back to the Mongol capital at Karakorum to participate in choosing a successor.

1243 Back on the warpath, but this time in the Middle East, the Mongols defeat the last remnants of the Seljuk Turks.

1248–54 King Louis IX of France (St. Louis) leads the Eighth Crusade, this time against the Mamluks, former slave soldiers who control Egypt. The result is the same: yet another defeat for the Europeans.

1260 The Mamluks become the first force to defeat the Mongols, in a battle at Goliath Spring in Palestine.

1260 Kublai Khan, greatest Mongol leader after his grandfather Genghis Khan, is declared Great Khan, or leader of the Mongols.

1261 Led by Michael VIII Palaeologus, the Byzantines re-capture Constantinople from the Latin Empire, and Byzantium enjoys one last gasp of power before it goes into terminal decline.

1270–72 In the Ninth Crusade, last of the numbered crusades, King Louis IX of France again leads the Europeans against the Mamluks, who defeat European forces yet again.

1271 **Marco Polo** embarks on his celebrated journey to the East, which lasts twenty-four years.

1279 Mongol forces under Kublai Khan win final victory over China's Sung dynasty. Thus begins the Yüan dynasty, the first time in Chinese history when the country has been ruled by foreigners.

1281 A Mongol force sent by Kublai Khan on a second attempt to take Japan—a first try, in 1274, also failed—is destroyed by a typhoon. The Japanese call it a "divine wind," or *kamikaze.*

1291 Mamluks conquer the last Christian stronghold at Acre, bringing to an end two centuries of crusades to conquer the Holy Land for Christendom.

1294 At the death of Kublai Khan, the Mongol realm is the largest empire in history, covering most of Asia and a large part of Europe. Actually it is four empires, including the Golden Horde in Russia; the Il-Khanate in the Middle East and Persia; Chagatai in Central Asia; and the Empire of the Great Khan, which includes China, Mongolia, and Korea. Within less than a century, however, this vast empire will have all but disappeared.

1300–1500 Era in European history often referred to as the Late Middle Ages.

1303 After years of conflict with Pope Boniface VIII, France's King Philip the Fair briefly has the pope arrested. This event and its aftermath marks the low point of the papacy during the Middle Ages.

1308 **Dante Alighieri** begins writing the *Divine Comedy,* which he will complete shortly before his death in 1321.

1309 Pope Clement V, an ally of Philip the Fair, moves the papal seat from Rome to Avignon in southern France.

1324 Mansa Musa, emperor of Mali, embarks on a pilgrimage to Mecca. After stopping in Cairo, Egypt, and spending so much gold that he affects the region's economy for years, he becomes famous throughout the Western world—the first sub-Saharan African ruler widely known among Europeans.

1337 England and France begin fighting what will become known as the Hundred Years' War, an on-again, off-again struggle to control parts of France.

1347–51 Europe experiences one of the worst disasters in human history, an epidemic called the Black Death. Sometimes called simply "the Plague," in four years the Black Death kills some thirty-five million people, or approximately one-third of the European population in 1300. The cause of the Plague can be traced to a bacteria carried by fleas, which in turn are borne by rats aboard ships arriving in Europe from Asia. Members of fanatical religious sects, however, claim that Jews started the epidemic by poisoning public water supplies. As a result of the anti-Semitic hysteria, many thousands of innocent people are murdered in addition to the millions dying from the Plague itself. Historian **Jacob von Königshofen** writes of one such massacre of Jews in the town of Strasbourg, a German-speaking city in what is now France.

1368 A group of Chinese rebels overthrows the Mongol Yüan dynasty and establishes the Ming dynasty, China's last native-born ruling house.

1378 The Catholic Church becomes embroiled in the Great Schism, which will last until 1417. During this time, there are rival popes in Rome and Avignon; and from 1409 to 1417, there is even a third pope in Pisa, Italy.

1386 Geoffrey Chaucer, heavily influenced by **Dante**, begins writing the *Canterbury Tales.*

1402 After conquering much of Iran and surrounding areas and then moving westward, Tamerlane defeats the Ottoman sultan Bajazed in battle. An unexpected result of their defeat is that the Ottomans, who seemed poised to take over much of Europe, go into a period of decline.

1404–05 Christine de Pisan, Europe's first female professional writer, publishes *The Book of the City of Ladies,* her most celebrated work.

1417 The Council of Constance ends the Great Schism, affirming that Rome is the seat of the church and that Pope Martin V is its sole leader. Unfortunately for the church, the Great Schism has weakened it at the very time that it faces its greatest challenge ever: a gathering movement that will come to be known as the Reformation.

1429 A tiny French army led by Joan of Arc forces the English to lift their siege on the town of Orléans, a victory that raises French spirits and makes it possible for France's king Charles VII to be crowned later that year. This marks a turning point in the Hundred Years' War.

1430–31 Captured by Burgundian forces, Joan of Arc is handed over to the English, who arrange her trial for witchcraft in a court of French priests. The trial, a mockery of justice, ends with Joan being burned at the stake.

1441 Fourteen black slaves are brought from Africa to Portugal, where they are presented to Prince Henry the Navigator. This is the beginning of the African slave trade, which isn't abolished until more than four centuries later.

1451 The recovery of the Ottoman Empire, which had suffered a half-century of decline, begins under Mehmet the Conqueror.

1453 Due in large part to the victories of Joan of Arc, which lifted French morale twenty-four years earlier, the Hundred Years' War ends with French victory.

1453 Turks under Mehmet the Conqueror march into Constantinople, bringing about the fall of the Byzantine Empire. Greece will remain part of the Ottoman Empire until 1829.

1455   Having developed a method of movable-type print-
        ing, Johannes Gutenberg of Mainz, Germany, prints
        his first book: a Bible. In the years to come, the inven-
        tion of the printing press will prove to be one of the
        most important events in world history. By making
        possible the widespread distribution of books, it will
        lead to increased literacy, which in turn creates a
        more educated, skilled, and wealthy populace. It will
        also influence the spread of local languages, and thus
        of national independence movements, and also spurs
        on the gathering movement for religious reformation.

1464   In the last-ever crusade, Pope Pius II attempts to re-
        take Turkish-held Constantinople for Christendom.
        However, he dies en route to Greece, bringing the cru-
        sading movement to an end.

1470   One of the first printed books to appear in England,
        La Morte D'Arthur by Sir Thomas Malory helps estab-
        lish the now-familiar tales of Arthurian legend.

1472   Ivan the Great of Muscovy marries Zoë, niece of the
        last Byzantine emperor, and adopts the two-headed
        Byzantine eagle as the symbol of Russia, the "Third
        Rome" after Rome itself and Byzantium. His grand-
        son, Ivan the Terrible, will in 1547 adopt the title *czar*,
        Russian for "caesar," title of Roman and Byzantine
        emperors for the past fifteen hundred years.

1492   Spain, united by the 1469 marriage of its two most
        powerful monarchs, Ferdinand II of Aragon and Is-
        abella I of Castile, drives out the last of the Muslims
        and expels all Jews. A less significant event of 1492,
        from the Spanish perspective, is the launch of a naval
        expedition in search of a westward sea route to China.
        Its leader is an Italian sailor named Christopher
        Columbus, who has grown up heavily influenced by
        Marco Polo's account of his travels.

1493   Mohammed I Askia takes the throne of Africa's Song-
        hai Empire, which will reach its height under his lead-
        ership.

1500   Date commonly cited as the end of Middle Ages, and
        the beginning of the Renaissance.

1517   Exactly a century after the Council of Constance ended the Great Schism, a German monk named Martin Luther publicly posts ninety-five theses, or statements challenging the established teachings of Catholicism, on the door of a church in Germany. Over the next century numerous new Protestant religious denominations will be established.

1550   The publication of *Description of Africa* by **Leo Africanus** gives most Europeans their first glimpse of sub-Saharan Africa, and the fame of Timbuktu—a city of scholars who prize books more than gold—spreads.

1591   Songhai, the last of the great premodern empires in Africa's Sudan region, falls to invaders from Morocco.

Words to Know

A

Age of Exploration: The period from about 1450 to about 1750, when European explorers conducted their most significant voyages and travels around the world.

Alchemy: A semi-scientific discipline that holds that through the application of certain chemical processes, ordinary metals can be turned into gold.

Algebra: A type of mathematics used to determine the value of unknown quantities where these can be related to known numbers.

Allegory: A type of narrative, popular throughout the Middle Ages, in which characters represent ideas.

Anarchy: Breakdown of political order.

Ancestor: An earlier person in one's line of parentage, usually more distant in time than a grandparent.

Anti-Semitism: Hatred of, or discrimination against, Jews.

Antipope: A priest proclaimed pope by one group or another, but not officially recognized by the church.

Archaeology: The scientific study of past civilizations.

Archbishop: The leading bishop in an area or nation.

Aristocracy: The richest and most powerful members of society.

Ascetic: A person who renounces all earthly pleasures as part of his or her search for religious understanding.

Assassination: Killing, usually of an important leader, for political reasons.

Astronomy: The scientific study of the stars and other heavenly bodies, and his or her movement in the sky.

B

Barbarian: A negative term used to describe someone as uncivilized.

Bishop: A figure in the Christian church assigned to oversee priests and believers in a given city or region.

Bureaucracy: A network of officials who run a government.

C

Caliph: A successor to Muhammad as spiritual and political leader of Islam.

Caliphate: The domain ruled by a caliph.

Canonization: Formal declaration of a deceased person as a saint.

Cardinal: An office in the Catholic Church higher than that of bishop or archbishop; the seventy cardinals in the "College of Cardinals" participate in electing the pope.

Cavalry: Soldiers on horseback.

Chivalry: The system of medieval knighthood, particularly its code of honor with regard to women.

Christendom: The Christian world.

Church: The entire Christian church, or more specifically the Roman Catholic Church.

City-state: A city that is also a self-contained political unit, like a country.

Civil service: The administrators and officials who run a government.

Civilization: A group of people possessing most or all of the following: a settled way of life, agriculture, a written language, an organized government, and cities.

Classical: Referring to ancient Greece and Rome.

Clergy: The priesthood.

Clerical: Relating to priests.

Coat of arms: A heraldic emblem representing a family or nation.

Commoner: Someone who is not a member of a royal or noble class.

Communion: The Christian ceremony of commemorating the last supper of Jesus Christ.

Courtly love: An idealized form of romantic love, usually of a knight or poet for a noble lady.

D

Dark Ages: A negative term sometimes used to describe the Early Middle Ages, the period from the fall of Rome to about A.D. 1000 in Western Europe.

Deity: A god.

Dialect: A regional variation on a language.

Diplomacy: The use of skillful negotiations with leaders of other nations to influence events.

Duchy: An area ruled by a duke, the highest rank of European noble below a prince.

Dynasty: A group of people, often but not always a family, who continue to hold a position of power over a period of time.

E

Economy: The whole system of production, distribution, and consumption of goods and services in a country.

Ecumenical: Across all faiths, or across all branches of the Christian Church.

Empire: A large political unit that unites many groups of people, often over a wide territory.

Epic: A long poem that recounts the adventures of a legendary hero.

Ethnic group: People who share a common racial, cultural, national, linguistic, or tribal origin.

Excommunicate: To banish someone from the church.

F

Famine: A food shortage caused by crop failures.

Fasting: Deliberately going without food, often but not always for religious reasons.

Feudalism: A form of political and economic organization in which peasants are subject to a noble who owns most or all of the land that they cultivate.

G

Geometry: A type of mathematics dealing with various shapes, their properties, and their measurements.

Guild: An association to promote, and set standards for, a particular profession or business.

H

Hajj: A pilgrimage to Mecca, which is expected of all Muslims who can afford to make it.

Heraldry: The practice of creating and studying coats of arms and other insignia.

Heresy: A belief that goes against established church teachings.

Holy Land: Palestine.

Horde: A division within the Mongol army; the term "hordes" was often used to describe the Mongol armies.

I

Icon: In the Christian church, an image of a saint.

Idol: A statue of a god that the god's followers worship.

Illumination: Decoration of a manuscript with elaborate designs.

Indo-European languages: The languages of Europe, India, Iran, and surrounding areas, which share common roots.

Indulgence: The granting of forgiveness of sins in exchange for an act of service for, or payment to, the church.

Infantry: Foot soldiers.

Infidel: An unbeliever.

Intellectual: A person whose profession or lifestyle centers around study and ideas.

Interest: In economics, a fee charged by a lender against a borrower—usually a percentage of the amount borrowed.

Investiture: The power of a feudal lord to grant lands or offices.

Islam: A religious faith that teaches submission to the one god Allah and his word as given through his prophet Muhammad in the Koran.

J

Jihad: Islamic "holy war" to defend or extend the faith.

K

Khan: A Central Asian chieftain.

Koran: The holy book of Islam.

L

Legal code: A system of laws.

Lingua franca: A common language.

M

Martyr: Someone who willingly dies for his or her faith.

Mass: A Catholic church service.

Medieval: Of or relating to the Middle Ages.

Middle Ages: Roughly the period from A.D. 500 to 1500.

Middle class: A group whose income level falls between that of the rich and the poor, or the rich and the working class; usually considered the backbone of a growing economy.

Millennium: A period of a thousand years.

Missionary: Someone who travels to other lands with the aim of converting others to his or her religion.

Monastery: A place in which monks live.

Monasticism: The tradition and practices of monks.

Monk: A man who leaves the outside world to take religious vows and live in a monastery, practicing a lifestyle of denying earthly pleasures.

Monotheism: Worship of one god.

Mosque: A Muslim temple.

Movable-type printing: An advanced printing process using pre-cast pieces of metal type.

Muezzin: A crier who calls worshipers to prayer five times a day in the Muslim world.

Mysticism: The belief that one can attain direct knowledge of God or ultimate reality through some form of meditation or special insight.

N

Nationalism: A sense of loyalty and devotion to one's nation.

Nation-state: A geographical area composed largely of a single nationality, in which a single national government clearly holds power.

New World: The Americas, or the Western Hemisphere.

Noble: A ruler within a kingdom who has an inherited title and lands, but who is less powerful than the king or queen; collectively, nobles are known as the *nobility.*

Nomadic: Wandering.

Novel: An extended, usually book-length, work of fiction.

Nun: The female equivalent of a monk, who lives in a nunnery, convent, or abbey.

O

Order: An organized religious community within the Catholic Church.

Ordination: Formal appointment as a priest or minister.

P

Pagan: Worshiping many gods.

Papacy: The office of the pope.

Papal: Referring to the pope.

Patriarch: A bishop in the Eastern Orthodox Church.

Patron: A supporter, particularly of arts, education, or sciences. The term is often used to refer to a ruler or wealthy person who provides economic as well as personal support.

Peasant: A farmer who works a small plot of land.

Penance: An act ordered by the church to obtain forgiveness for sin.

Persecutions: In early church history, Roman punishment of Christians for their faith.

Philosophy: An area of study concerned with subjects including values, meaning, and the nature of reality.

Pilgrimage: A journey to a site of religious significance.

Plague: A disease that spreads quickly to a large population.

Polytheism: Worship of many gods.

Pope: The bishop of Rome, and therefore the head of the Catholic Church.

Principality: An area ruled by a prince, the highest-ranking form of noble below a king.

Prophet: Someone who receives communications directly from God and passes these on to others.

Prose: Written narrative, as opposed to poetry.

Purgatory: A place of punishment after death where, according to Roman Catholic beliefs, a person who has not been damned may work out his or her salvation and earn his or her way to heaven.

R

Rabbi: A Jewish teacher or religious leader.

Racism: The belief that race is the primary factor determining peoples' abilities and that one race is superior to another.

Reason: The use of the mind to figure things out; usually contrasted with emotion, intuition, or faith.

Reformation: A religious movement in the 1500s that ultimately led to the rejection of Roman Catholicism by various groups who adopted Protestant interpretations of Christianity.

Regent: Someone who governs a country when the monarch is too young, too old, or too sick to lead.

Relic: An object associated with the saints of the New Testament, or the martyrs of the early church.

Renaissance: A period of renewed interest in learning and the arts that began in Europe during the 1300s and continued to the 1600s.

Representational art: Artwork intended to show a specific subject, whether a human figure, landscape, still life, or a variation on these.

Ritual: A type of religious ceremony that is governed by very specific rules.

Rome: A term sometimes used to refer to the papacy.

S

Sack: To destroy, usually a city.

Saracen: A negative term used in medieval Europe to describe Muslims.

Scientific method: A means of drawing accurate conclusions by collecting information, studying data, and forming theories or hypotheses.

Scriptures: Holy texts.

Sect: A small group within a larger religion.

Secular: Of the world; typically used in contrast to "spiritual."

Semitic: A term describing a number of linguistic and cultural groups in the Middle East, including the modern-day Arabs and Israelis.

Serf: A peasant subject to a feudal system and possessing no land.

Siege: A sustained military attack against a city.

Simony: The practice of buying and selling church offices.

Sultan: A type of king in the Muslim world.

Sultanate: An area ruled by a Sultan.

Synagogue: A Jewish temple.

T

Technology: The application of knowledge to make the performance of physical and mental tasks easier.

Terrorism: Frightening (and usually harming) a group of people in order to achieve a specific political goal.

Theologian: Someone who analyzes religious faith.

Theology: The study of religious faith.

Trial by ordeal: A system of justice in which the accused (and sometimes the accuser as well) has to undergo various physical hardships in order to prove innocence.

Tribal: Describes a society, sometimes nomadic, in which members are organized by families and clans, not by region, and in which leadership comes from warrior-chieftains.

Tribute: Forced payments to a conqueror.

Trigonometry: The mathematical study of triangles, angles, arcs, and their properties and applications.

Trinity: The three persons of God according to Christianity—Father, Son, and Holy Spirit.

U

Usury: Loaning money for a high rate of interest; during the Middle Ages, however, it meant simply loaning money for interest.

V

Vassal: A noble or king who is subject to a more powerful noble or king.

Vatican: The seat of the pope's power in Rome.

W

West: Generally, Western Europe and North America, or the countries influenced both by ancient Greece and ancient Rome.

Working class: A group between the middle class and the poor who typically earn a living with their hands.

Cultures in Conflict

People often have a difficult time accepting other groups, and this was certainly the case in the medieval period, when nations clung fiercely to their religions and ways of life. The difficulties of travel also made it unlikely that people would come into regular contact with outsiders—except in the highly undesirable circumstance of an invasion or attack.

From the A.D. 300s, as the Western Roman Empire began to crumble, parts of Europe sustained waves of attacks by various invaders; however, the Eastern Roman Empire, better known as the Byzantine (BIZ-un-teen) Empire, continued to thrive in Greece. In 1071, however, the Byzantines suffered a stunning defeat by the Turks, a formerly nomadic or wandering tribe from Central Asia that had settled in Anatolia (modern-day Turkey). As a result, in 1095 the Byzantine emperor called for help from Western Europe.

East-West relations in Europe had long been strained, with the Byzantines regarding the Westerners as uncouth, and the Westerners viewing the Byzantines as arrogant or proud. The groups even adopted separate forms of Christianity: Roman Catholicism under the leadership of the pope in the West, and Greek Orthodoxy in the East. The split became official in 1054—but now the Byzantines hoped to rally Christian support against the Turks, who were Muslims.

As it turned out, the Byzantines got more than they bargained for. The Byzantine princess **Anna Comnena** (kahm-NEE-nuh; c. 1083–1148) made this clear in her history of her father's reign, which portrayed the "Gauls"—a derisive or mocking nickname used for Western Europeans—as foolish, greedy thugs. Anna revealed a perhaps typical Byzantine viewpoint with her obvious contempt for the Westerners as inferiors of the Greeks.

Given the much more advanced civilization of the Byzantines, it is understandable that she would feel that way, especially because it soon became clear that the "Gauls" were more interested in helping themselves than in helping the Byzantines. Instead of saving the Byzantine Empire, the pope and other Western leaders launched the Crusades, a series of wars intended to seize the Holy Land, or Palestine, from the Muslims who controlled it.

In Palestine, the Westerners rubbed shoulders with Arabs such as **Usamah ibn Munqidh** (oo-SAH-muh EEB'n moon-KEED; 1095–1188), who, like their Byzantine counterparts, regarded the Western Europeans—he called them "Franks"—as inferiors. Likewise Usamah's belief in the superiority of his civilization is understandable: at a time when few Western Europeans could read and write, Muslim culture enjoyed tremendous advances in science, mathematics, and the arts.

The Muslims, for their part, were also experienced invaders of other lands: in 1080, just before the Crusades began, armies from Morocco wiped out the splendid West African empire of Ghana (GAHN-uh). Just a few years before, according to the Muslim traveler **Al-Bekri** (beh-KREE), Ghana had seemed secure in its wealth and power, but already the introduction of the Islamic or Muslim faith posed a challenge to the people's traditions. Farther south was Timbuktu, still a great center of learning when **Leo Africanus** (c. 1485–c. 1554) visited it in about 1526; but later wars between neighboring tribes would bring its glories to an end.

Leo's record of his travels provided Europeans with a rare glimpse of premodern Africa, and inspired fascination with the exotic lands beyond the Sahara Desert. Similarly, **Marco Polo** (1254–1324) caused a great stir with his account of an even more distant place: China. Because of natural barriers separating them from the rest of the world, until the A.D. 100s the Chinese had assumed they were the only civilized people; the only other groups they knew of were "barbarian" tribes on their northern borders. By the time Marco visited in the late 1200s, the "barbarian" Mongols had conquered China, and his recollections carry hints of Chinese resentment toward the invaders.

Like the Crusades in the Holy Land, which ended in 1291, the Mongol conquests helped spur Europe into a new age of change and discovery. As the Roman Empire had once done, the empire of the Mongols united much of the world under one rule. The Mongols suppressed many tribes and rulers who might have threatened people traveling through their realms, and thus for the first time in centuries, travel between Europe and Asia was relatively safe and easy. But the opening up of the world also made possible an entirely new kind of invasion: one by bacteria or microscopic organism. Carried by fleas who lived in the fur of rats, the Black Death or Plague (1347–51) wiped out as much as forty-five percent of Europe. Many Europeans blamed Jews for causing the Black Death. A passage from the writings of **Jacob von Königshofen** on this subject provides a particularly unsettling example of cultures in conflict.

Anna Comnena

Excerpt from **The Alexiad**
Published in *The First Crusade:*
***The Accounts of Eyewitnesses and Participants,* 1921**

The Byzantine (BIZ-un-teen) Empire—sometimes referred to as "Byzantium" (bi-ZAN-tee-um)—was a continuation of the ancient Roman Empire. In fact, the Byzantines referred to themselves as "Romans" rather than using the term Byzantine, which referred to the old name of their capital in Greece. In A.D. 330, the center of Byzantium had become Constantinople (kahn-stan-ti-NOH-pul), capital of the Eastern Roman Empire.

After the fall of the Western Roman Empire in 476, Byzantium became more and more separated from Western Europe. This led to a division of faiths, with Western Europe adhering to Latin Christianity, or Roman Catholicism, and Eastern Europe accepting the Greek Orthodox Church. Many differences developed, with Catholics taking their leadership from the pope while members of the Orthodox Church increasingly charted a separate course. In 1054, the Latin and Greek churches officially separated.

Three years later, the Comnenus (kahm-NEEN-us) family assumed the Byzantine throne and established a dynasty, or royal line of succession, that would last for many centuries. But these were troubled times for the empire: in

> "Alexius was not yet, or very slightly, rested from his labors when he heard rumors of the arrival of innumerable Frankish armies."

5

Anna Comnena

Anna Comnena was the eldest
daughter of Byzantine emperor Alexis I
Comnenus. In 1097, when she was fourteen, she married thirty-year-old Nicephorus Bryennius (ny-SEF-ur-us bry-EN-ee-us;
1067–1137). Nicephorus was a historian
and a learned man, and Anna, who received the best education available, would
eventually become the world's first notable
female historian.

Though the Byzantines had been
ruled by females before, Anna knew that
her chances of taking the throne were slim,
particularly because she had a younger
brother, John. Yet in 1118, when she was
thirty-five, she made an unsuccessful bid to
place Nicephorus on the throne. John defeated the plot and went on to rule as John
II for the next twenty-five years, while Anna
spent the rest of her life in a monastery, a
secluded place for people who have taken
religious vows.

There she wrote the *Alexiad,* a history of the period from 1069 to 1118—that is,

Anna Comnena. *Reproduced by permission of the
Library of Congress.*

from the time her uncle, Isaac Comnenus,
established the dynasty to the end of her father's reign. The suffix -*ad* usually means
that a work is the glorious tale of a nation,
and certainly Anna's history provides an
image of the Byzantine Empire under her
family's rule as a highly civilized realm.

1071, the Byzantines suffered a crippling defeat by the Turks
at the Battle of Manzikert in Armenia. Therefore in 1095, Emperor Alexis I Comnenus (ruled 1081–1118) asked Pope Urban
II (ruled 1088–99) to send assistance in the form of troops.

Despite Alexis's request for help, divisions between
Byzantines and Western Europeans remained severe. The
Byzantines rightly viewed their own civilization as more advanced than that of the westerners, who they lumped together as "Latins," "Gauls," or "Franks." The last two were the

names of two tribes who had once controlled parts of the West, and the use of these terms implied that the Western Europeans were barbarians, or uncivilized. Indeed, the term "barbarian" was often used by the Byzantines and their ancient Greek ancestors to describe all non-Greeks.

The Byzantines did not simply look down on the "Franks"—they were also afraid of them, and with good reason. In 1081, a group of Normans—descendants of the Vikings who had earlier terrorized much of Europe—had tried to invade Byzantine territories. Leading the attack was Robert Guiscard (gee-SKARD; c. 1015–1085), aided by his son Bohemond I (BOH-ay-maw; c. 1050–1111). Thus Alexis became alarmed when he learned that huge numbers of Western Europeans were headed east—and that Bohemond was at the head of one army. Later, Alexis's daughter Anna Comnena (c. 1083–1148) would compose an official history of her father's reign, the *Alexiad* (uh-LEX-ee-ad). In it, she would write of events that occurred when she was in her early teens, when her father was faced with an unwelcome visit from Bohemond in 1096.

Things to remember while reading the excerpt from *The Alexiad*

- Like many Byzantines, Anna looked down on Western Europeans, whom she referred to by the uncomplimentary nickname of "Gauls." She also called them "Latins," which was not as negative. Ill-will was particularly strong against Bohemond and the Normans, who had tried to invade the Byzantine Empire just fifteen years before.

- Durazzo (dü-RAT-soh) was a city in what is now Albania, which the Normans attempted to take from the Byzantines in 1081. Larissa is an area in Greece, and Cosmidion was a Greek city.

- It was common in pre-modern times for kings and other leaders to employ food-tasters, men whose job it was to taste the king's food and drinks and thus ensure that these were not poisoned.

- Because of differences in language, Anna Comnena renders the name of her father as "Alexius" rather than Alexis, and that of Bohemond as "Bohemund."

Excerpt from The Alexiad

... But when Bohemund had arrived ... with his companions, realizing both that he was not of noble birth, and that for lack of money he had not brought with him a large enough army, he hastened, with only ten Gauls, ahead of the other **counts** *and arrived at Constantinople. He did this to win the favor of the Emperor for himself, and to conceal more safely the plans which he was concocting against him. Indeed, the Emperor, to whom the schemes of the man were known, for he had long since become acquainted with the hidden and* **deceitful** *dealings of this same Bohemund, took great pains to arrange it so that before the other counts should come he would speak with him alone. Thus having heard what Bohemund had to say, he hoped to persuade him to cross before the others came, lest, joined with them after their coming, he might* **pervert** *their minds.*

When Bohemund had come to him, the Emperor greeted him with gladness and inquired anxiously about the journey and where he had left his companions. Bohemund responded to all these things as he thought best for his own interests, **affably** *and in a friendly way, while the Emperor recalled in a familiar talk his bold undertakings long ago around Durazzo and Larissa and the hostilities between them at that time. Bohemund answered, "Then I confess I was your enemy, then I was hostile. But, behold, I now stand before you like a deserter to the ranks of the enemy! I am a friend of your Majesty." The Emperor proceeded to* **scrutinize** *the man, considering him cautiously and carefully and drawing out what was in his mind. As soon as he saw that Bohemund was ready to consent to swear an oath of* **fealty** *to him, he said, "You must be tired from the journey and should retire to rest. We will talk tomorrow about anything else."*

So Bohemund departed ... to Cosmidion, where hospitality was found, a table richly laden.... Then the cooks came and showed him the uncooked flesh of animals and birds, saying: "We have prepared this food which you see on the table according to our skill and the custom of this region; but if, perchance, these please you less, here is food, still uncooked, which can be prepared just as you order." The Emperor, because of his almost incredible **tact** *in handling men, had commanded that this be done and said by them. For, since he was especially expert in penetrating the secrets of minds and in discover-*

Counts: Relatively low-ranking noblemen.

Deceitful: Dishonest.

Pervert (v.): Corrupt.

Affably: In a cheerful manner.

Scrutinize: Study carefully.

Fealty: Loyalty.

Tact: Skill in knowing what to say and do so as to maintain good relations with other people.

ing the **disposition** of a man, he very readily understood that Bohemund was of a **shrewd** and suspicious nature; and he foresaw what happened. For, lest Bohemund should conceive any suspicion against him, the Emperor had ordered that raw meats be placed before him, together with the cooked, thus easily removing suspicion. Neither did his conjecture fail, for the very shrewd Bohemund took the prepared food, without even touching it with the tips of his fingers, or tasting it, and immediately turned around, concealing, nevertheless, the suspicion which occurred to him by the following **ostentatious** show of **liberality**. For under the pretext of courtesy he distributed all the food to those standing around; in reality, if one understood rightly, he was dividing the cup of death among them. Nor did he conceal his cunning, so much did he hold his subjects in contempt; for he this day used the raw meat which had been offered to him and had it prepared by his own cooks after the

Alexis I Comnenus ruled the Byzantine Empire from 1081 to 1118. *Reproduced by permission of the Library of Congress.*

manner of his country. On the next day he asked his men whether they were well. Upon their answering in the **affirmative**, that they were indeed very well, that not even one felt even the least indisposed, he **disclosed** his secret in his reply: "Remembering a war, once carried on by me against the Emperor, and that strife, I feared lest perchance he had intended to kill me by putting deadly poison in my food."

... After this, the Emperor saw to it that a room in the palace was so filled with a collection of riches of all kinds that the very floor was covered with costly **raiment**, and with gold and silver coins, and certain other less valuable things, so much so that one was not able even to walk there, so hindered was he by the abundance of these things. The Emperor ordered the guide suddenly and unexpectedly to open the doors, thus revealing all this to Bohemund. Amazed at the spectacle, Bohemund exclaimed: "If such riches were mine, long ago I would have been lord of many lands!" The guide answered, "And all these things the Emperor **bestows** upon you today as a gift." Most gladly Bohemund received them and with many gracious

Disposition: Attitude.

Shrewd: Clever.

Ostentatious: Conspicuous, like a show-off.

Liberality: Generosity.

Affirmative: Positive—i.e., yes.

Disclosed: Revealed.

Raiment: Clothing.

Bestows: Gives.

Ignominy: Humiliating or disgraceful conduct.

Base (adj.): Low.

Surpassing: Above everyone or everything else.

Malice: Bad intentions.

Intrepidity: Fearlessness.

Inconstant: Unpredictable, changing.

Spurned: Rejected.

Pretext: A reason one claims for doing something, when in fact the real reason is secret— and usually less admirable.

Lord's Sepulchre: The place in Jerusalem where Jesus was said to have been buried.

*thanks he left, intending to return to his rest in the inn. But changing his mind when they were brought to him, he, who a little before had admired them, said: "Never can I let myself be treated with such **ignominy** by the Emperor. Go, take those things and carry them back to him who sent them." The Emperor, knowing the **base** fickleness of the Latins, quoted this common saying, "Let the evil return to its author." Bohemund having heard this, and seeing that the messengers were busily bringing these things back to him, decided anew about the goods which he had sent back with regret, and ... changed in a moment.... For he was quick, and a man of very dishonest disposition, as much **surpassing** in **malice** and **intrepidity** all the Latins who had crossed over as he was inferior to them in power and wealth. But even though he thus excelled all in great cunning, the **inconstant** character of the Latins was also in him. Verily, the riches which he **spurned** at first, he now gladly accepted. For when this man of evil design had left his country in which he possessed no wealth at all (under the **pretext**, indeed, of adoring at the **Lord's Sepulchre**, but in reality endeavoring to acquire for himself a kingdom), he found himself in need of much money, especially, indeed, if he was to seize the Roman power. In this he followed the advice of his father and, so to speak, was leaving no stone unturned.*

What happened next...

By the time of Bohemond's arrival in Constantinople, the original purpose of the expedition from the West had been lost; 1095 marked the beginning of the Crusades, a series of wars in which popes and rulers in Western Europe attempted to seize control of the Holy Land (Palestine) from the Muslim Turks. The First Crusade, which resulted in the capture of Jerusalem and other cities, would mark the high point of this effort.

Bohemond became ruler over one of those captured cities, Antioch, yet he did not stop when he was ahead. First he was captured by the Turks in a failed attack on another city in 1099, then in 1107 he launched an unsuccessful attack against his old foe Alexis. Alexis got the better of him, more through superior mental skill than through the use of his

Crusading peasants and troops. Alexis's enemy Bohemond fought in the First Crusade in between attempts to overthrow the Byzantine Empire.
Reproduced by permission of the New York Public Library Picture Collection.

armies, and forced Bohemond to sign a treaty in which he recognized Alexis as the superior ruler.

The Crusades themselves, which continued until 1291, were a disaster for Byzantium. The Fourth Crusade (1202–04) ended with the capture of Constantinople by Western Europeans, and the establishment of the so-called Latin Empire. The Comnenus family went on to rule a breakaway

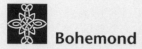

Bohemond

Bohemond I—his name can also be spelled "Bohemund," as Anna Comnena rendered it—was a member of a group called the Normans, descendants of the Vikings. He had grown up fighting in the army of his father Robert Guiscard (gee-SKARD; c. 1015–1085), who drove the forces of the Byzantine Empire from Italy and later conquered Sicily, a large island off the Italian coast. In 1081, Robert and Bohemond launched a series of unsuccessful campaigns against the Byzantines in southeastern Europe.

In 1096, Bohemond joined the First Crusade (1095–99), an effort to seize control of the Holy Land, or Palestine, from the Muslim Turks. In 1098 he led the crusaders in the capture of Antioch (AN-tee-ahk), a city on the border between Turkey and Syria, and went on to become ruler of Antioch. In the following year, however, he engaged in an unsuccessful attempt to take another Muslim-controlled city, and was captured by the Turks.

Released in 1103, Bohemond returned to Europe, where he tried to gather support for another campaign against the Byzantines. By now he was well into his fifties and unmarried, but in 1106, King Philip I of France gave him the hand of his daughter Constance—an important match for Bohemond. Confident in the support of his powerful father-in-law, he went on to make war against the Byzantines in 1107, but failed to gain victory.

Byzantine state called Trebizond, which lasted until 1461. In the meantime, the Byzantines recaptured Constantinople in 1261, but they had been so badly weakened that they were easily defeated by the Ottoman Turks in 1453. The Turks gave Constantinople its present name of Istanbul.

Did you know ...

- Anna Comnena wrote of one unnamed prince of the "Franks" who was so uncouth that he sat down on Emperor Alexis's throne. When one of his wiser comrades suggested he move, he said of Alexis, "This must be a rude fellow who would alone remain seated when so many brave warriors are standing up." Anna said that when he learned of this, Alexis "did not complain ... although he did not forget the matter."

- Despite his bad relations with most of the Western European leaders, Alexis took a deep and genuine liking to Raymond of Toulouse (tuh-LOOS; 1042–1105). The emperor took the young French count, destined for glory in the Crusades, under his wing and warned him to steer clear of Bohemond. Anna wrote of Raymond, "He was as far superior to all the Latins ... as the sun is above the other stars."

For More Information

Books

Barrett, Tracy. *Anna of Byzantium.* New York: Delacorte Press, 1999.

Anna Comnena. *The Alexiad of the Princess Anna Comnena: Being the History of the Reign of Her Father, Alexius I, Emperor of the Romans, 1081–1118 A.D.* Translated by Elizabeth A. S. Dawes. New York: AMS Press, 1978.

Encyclopedia of World Biography, second edition. Detroit: Gale, 1998.

Krey, August C. *The First Crusade: The Accounts of Eyewitnesses and Participants.* Princeton, NJ: Princeton University Press, 1921.

Web Sites

"Medieval Sourcebook: Anna Comnena: *The Alexiad:* On the Crusades." *Medieval Sourcebook.* [Online] Available http://www.fordham.edu/halsall/source/comnena-cde.html (last accessed July 28, 2000).

Usamah ibn Munqidh

Excerpt from **The Memoirs of Usamah ibn Munqidh**
**Published in *An Arab-Syrian Gentleman and Warrior in the Period of
the Crusades: Memoirs of Usamah ibn Munqidh*, 1987**

In 1095, armies from Western Europe marched on Palestine, intent on gaining control of the Holy Land—that is, the area where most of the events recorded in the Bible took place. Standing in their way were the Muslims who controlled the area. The Muslim or Islamic faith has much in common with Christianity and Judaism, including its respect for many of the people and places referred to in the Old and New testaments.

For centuries, Christians who wanted to visit the holy sites had done so without interference, but once the area came under the control of the Turks, a people who came ultimately from the grasslands of Central Asia, things began to change. Not only were the Turks less willing to allow Christian pilgrims to enter the Holy Land, but European leaders—including the pope, the leader of Roman Catholic Christianity—desired to gain control of Palestine for themselves.

The First Crusade (1095–99) ended in success for the Europeans, with the capture of Jerusalem and the establishment of four European-controlled "crusader" states throughout the area of modern-day Israel, Lebanon, and Syria. Many

"When one comes to recount cases regarding the Franks, he cannot but glorify Allah (exalted is he!) and sanctify him, for he sees them as animals possessing the virtues of courage and fighting, but nothing else."

Usamah ibn Munqidh

The story of the Crusades, the "holy wars" by which Western Europeans tried to gain control of Palestine, is usually told from the perspective of the European invaders. Thus the autobiography or life story written by Usamah ibn Munqidh, a Muslim defender, offers a fresh perspective.

Usamah served as a soldier and administrator under Nur ad-Din (NOOR ed-DEEN; 1118–1174), the sultan or ruler of Egypt and Syria. After living in Egypt for a time, he returned to his home in Palestine and asked the sultan for his permission to move his family back. Nur ad-Din agreed, and arranged a letter of safe passage, which should have guaranteed that the family's ship would face no danger from the European invaders. Indeed, Usamah recalled that "the Frankish king"—the leader of the Europeans in the region—had

agreed to the safe passage. But when the ship neared its destination, a group of European pirates attacked the ship with the blessings of the "Frankish king."

The pirates robbed Usamah's family of almost everything. Later he wrote, "Compared with the safety of my sons, my brother, and our women, the loss of the rest meant little to me, except for my books. There had been 4,000 fine volumes on board, and their destruction has been a cruel loss to me for the rest of my life." Usamah had a long life in which to remember: at a time when the average life expectancy in Western Europe was no more than thirty years, he lived to the ripe old age of ninety-three. Despite his bad experiences with the "Franks," he developed many friendships with Europeans, as he recounted in his autobiography, written about 1175.

of the Muslims who lived in the region, who were Arab rather than Turkish, looked down on the Western Europeans and, like the Byzantines of Greece, referred to them as "Franks." Again like the Byzantines, the Arabs viewed the "Franks" from the perspective of their own highly developed civilization, which had yielded enormous progress in science, mathematics, and the arts over the preceding centuries.

The "Franks" may have been unwashed barbarians, or uncivilized people, in the view of the Arabs, but in the time of Usamah ibn Munqidh (oo-SAH-muh EEB'n moon-KEED; 1095–1188), it seemed that they were there to stay. By then, the principal Muslim force in the Middle East was no longer the Turks; rather, power had shifted to the Fatimid dynasty in

Egypt, under which Usamah served as a soldier and administrator. In his *Memoirs*, or life story, Usamah offered a fascinating portrait of the uneasy relationship between the Arabs and the Christians who had settled in Palestine.

Things to remember while reading the excerpt from *The Memoirs of Usamah ibn Munqidh*

- Usamah's account presents a rare view of medieval medical practice—if such a term can be applied to the ghastly practices in Western Europe at the time. His story of the knight's leg and the insane woman's skull is not for the faint of heart, but it is probably all too accurate, and it illustrates the fact that European "doctors" often blamed diseases on spiritual rather than physical causes. To Usamah, these practices must have seemed particularly backward, because Arab doctors were among the most highly advanced in the medieval world.

Arab astronomers. Compared to Western Europe, Arab civilizations were very advanced in scientific fields in the Middle Ages. *Reproduced by permission of the New York Public Library Picture Collection.*

- The reference to making the woman's "humor wet" implies the medieval belief in humors, or bodily fluids such as blood. It appears that Thabit (tah-BEET), the Christian physician referred to—who was probably not a "Frank" but someone from the Middle East—simply intended to get her circulation going, which was probably not a bad idea.

- In another passage, Usamah expressed amazement at the Europeans' relatively open-minded attitudes toward "their" women. In the Muslim world, a man was undisputed master in his house, and most Islamic men of wealth such as Usamah had more than one wife. Thus although attitudes toward women in medieval Europe would hardly be considered forward-thinking by modern standards, to Usamah they were amazing.

- Usamah's observations on the Europeans are colored by his obviously low view of them, which is particularly interesting because Europeans in later centuries would themselves view other peoples, including Arabs, as their inferiors. This attitude was not necessarily the same as hatred, however: Usamah compared the "Franks" to animals that could be either pleasant or unruly depending on how they were handled.

- Not all the place names in this passage are clear; however, it is known that "Sur" was Tyre (TIRE), an ancient city in what is now Lebanon; and that Nablus (NAH-blus) is in the modern nation of Jordan.

Excerpt from
Memoirs of Usamah ibn Munqidh

The lord of al-Munaytirah wrote to my uncle asking him to dispatch a physician to treat certain sick persons among his people. My uncle sent him a Christian physician named Thabit. Thabit was absent but ten days when he returned. So we said to him, "How quickly has thou healed thy patients!" He said:

*"They brought before me a knight in whose leg an **abscess** had grown; and a woman afflicted with **imbecility**. To the knight I ap-*

Abscess: A sore characterized by pus and inflamed tissue.

Imbecility: Idiocy; in this case, it means insanity.

plied a small **poultice** until the abscess opened and became well; and the woman I put on diet and made her **humor** wet. Then a Frankish physician came to them and said, 'This man knows nothing about treating them.' He then said to the knight, 'Which wouldst thou prefer, living with one leg or dying with two?' The latter replied, 'Living with one leg.' The physician said, 'Bring me a strong knight and a sharp ax.' A knight came with the ax. And I was standing by. Then the physician laid the leg of the patient on a block of wood and **bade** the knight strike his leg with the ax and chop it off at one blow. Accordingly he struck it—while I was looking on—one blow, but the leg was not severed. He dealt another blow, upon which the **marrow** of the leg flowed out and the patient died on the spot. He then examined the woman and said, 'This is a woman in whose head there is a devil which has possessed her. Shave off her hair.' Accordingly they shaved it off and the woman began once more to eat their ordinary diet—garlic and mustard. Her imbecility took a turn for the worse. The physician then said, 'The devil has penetrated through her head.' He therefore took a razor, made a deep **cruciform** incision on it, peeled off the skin at the middle of the incision until the bone of the skull was exposed and rubbed it with salt. The woman also **expired** instantly. Thereupon I asked them whether my services were needed any longer, and when they replied in the negative I returned home, having learned of their medicine what I knew not before."

I have, however, witnessed a case of their medicine which was quite different from that.

The king of the Franks had for treasurer a knight named Bernard, who (may Allah's curse be upon him!) was one of the most accursed and wicked among the Franks. A horse kicked him in the leg, which was subsequently infected and which opened in fourteen different places. Every time one of these cuts would close in one place, another would open in another place. All this happened while I was praying for his **perdition**. Then came to him a Frankish physician and removed from the leg all the ointments which were on it and began to wash it with very strong vinegar. By this treatment all the cuts were healed and the man became well again. He was up again like a devil....

The Franks are **void** of all zeal and jealousy. One of them may be walking along with his wife. He meets another man who takes the wife by the hand and steps aside to converse with her while the husband is standing on one side waiting for his wife to conclude the

Poultice: Medicated cloth applied to a wound or sore.

Humor: A medieval term for bodily fluids such as blood.

Bade: Commanded.

Marrow: Tissue inside of bones.

Cruciform: In the shape of a cross.

Expired: Died.

Perdition: Destruction.

Void: Without.

*conversation. If she lingers too long for him, he leaves her alone with
the conversant and goes away.*

Here is an illustration which I myself witnessed:

*When I used to visit Nablus, I always took lodging with a man
named Mu'izz, whose home was a lodging house for the Muslims.
The house had windows which opened to the road, and there stood
opposite to it on the other side of the road a house belonging to a
Frank who sold wine for the merchants. He would take some wine in
a bottle and go around announcing it by shouting, "So and so, the
merchant, has just opened a cask full of this wine. He who wants to
buy some of it will find it in such and such a place." The Frank's pay
for the announcement made would be the wine in that bottle. One
day this Frank went home and found a man with his wife in the
same bed. He asked him, "What could have made you enter into my
wife's room?" The man replied, "I was tired, so I went in to rest."
"But how," asked he, "didst thou get into my bed?" The other
replied, "I found a bed that was spread, so I slept in it." "But," said*

Middle Ages: Primary Sources

he, "my wife was sleeping together with you!" The other replied, "Well, the bed is hers. How could I therefore have prevented her from using her own bed?"

"By the truth of my religion," said the husband, "if thou shouldst do it again, thou and I would have a quarrel." Such was for the Frank the entire expression of his disapproval and the limit of his jealousy....

Another illustration: I entered the public bath in Sur and took my place in a secluded part. One of my servants thereupon said to me, "There is with us in the bath a woman." When I went out, I sat on one of the stone benches and behold! the woman who was in the bath had come out all dressed and was standing with her father just opposite me. But I could not be sure that she was a woman. So I said to one of my companions, "By Allah, see if this is a woman," by which I meant that he should ask about her. But he went, as I was looking at him, lifted the end of her robe and looked carefully at her. Thereupon her father turned toward me and said, "This is my daughter. Her mother is dead and she has nobody to wash her hair. So I took her in with me to the bath and washed her head." I replied, "Thou hast well done! This is something for which thou shalt be rewarded [by Allah]!"

What happened next ...

The "Franks" may have thought they were in the Holy Land to stay, but events of later years would prove them wrong. In Usamah's lifetime, they had already lost ground, and though they enjoyed some success in the Third Crusade, which began the year after he died in 1188, this success was short-lived.

By the 1200s, the crusading spirit had begun to die out. The primary target of the Fourth Crusade (1202–04) turned out not to be the Muslims, but Christians in the Byzantine Empire. Later crusades involved a number of colorful figures, but the results were less and less impressive. In 1291, the last crusader stronghold in Acre (AHK-ruh) fell.

Did you know ...

- Although Crusades in the Holy Land came to an end in 1291, Europeans continued to wage "holy wars"—against Muslims and supposed enemies of the faith at home—up until 1464. The last crusade was an attempt to recapture the Byzantine Empire from the Turks, who had destroyed it eleven years before; ironically, the Western Europeans' Crusades had played a major role in weakening Byzantium and leaving it open to invasion.

- Though he maintained a generally low view of the "Franks," Usamah ibn Munqidh considered some of them friends, and even gave some of them his grudging respect—as his account of the European doctor's successful treatment of the knight Bernard illustrates. Elsewhere in his *Memoirs,* he reports on a generous European host who understood the ways of the Muslims enough to assure his guests that no pork (which is forbidden by the Islamic religion) was ever served at his table.

For More Information

Books

Gabriell, Francesco. *Arab Historians of the Crusades.* Berkeley, CA: University of California Press, 1964.

Usamah ibn Munqidh. *An Arab-Syrian Gentleman and Warrior in the Period of the Crusades: Memoirs of Usamah ibn Munqidh.* Translated by Philip K. Hitti. Princeton, NJ: Princeton University Press, 1987.

Web Sites

"Islam and Islamic History in Arabia and the Middle East." *IslamiCity in Cyberspace.* [Online] Available http://www.islam.org/mosque/ihame/Sec10.htm (last accessed July 28, 2000).

"Medieval Sourcebook: Usamah ibn Munqidh (1095–1188): *Autobiography,* Excerpts on the Franks." *Medieval Sourcebook.* [Online] Available http://www.fordham.edu/halsall/source/usamah2.html (last accessed July 28, 2000).

Al-Bekri

Excerpt from Al-Masalik wa 'l-Mamalik
Published in *African Civilization Revisited,* **1991**

Leo Africanus

Excerpt from Description of Africa
Published in *Readings about the World, Volume 2,* **1999**

The Sahara Desert in Africa is larger than the continental United States. Not surprisingly, this most forbidding of all deserts ensured that the southern part of the African continent would be shut off from the northern part, where the people had much greater opportunities for communication with other lands. Some of the most notable civilizations of premodern Africa, however, arose on the edges of the Sahara.

Among these was Ghana (GAH-nuh), which reached its high point in the A.D. 1000s. Ghana became incredibly wealthy and powerful, largely on the strength of its enormous gold reserves. Another important center of civilization was the city of Timbuktu, which flourished under the empires of Mali (MAHL-ee) and Songhai (SAWNG-hy) during the 1300s and 1400s. So many scholars lived in Timbuktu that, according to Leo Africanus (c. 1485–c. 1554), books were the most highly prized items sold in the markets there.

Yet despite Ghana's riches in gold, and the intellectual wealth of Timbuktu, both were in a highly fragile situation. From the description of Ghana written by al-Bekri (beh-KREE) in about 1067, it is hard to imagine that the splendid empire

"The king of Ghana can put two hundred thousand warriors in the field, more than forty thousand being armed with bow and arrow."

From Al-Masalik wa 'l-Mamalik

"Many hand-written books imported from Barbary are also sold [in the market at Timbuktu]. There is more profit made from this commerce than from all other merchandise."

From Description of Africa

Al-Bekri and Leo Africanus

Little is known about al-Bekri, except that he was a Muslim from Spain who visited West Africa in about 1067. The record of his travels, *Al-Masalik wa 'l-Mamalik,* has not even been translated into English; instead, the version included here comes from author Basil Davidson's English rendering of a passage from a French translation.

Leo Africanus is more well known. Like al-Bekri, he was a Muslim from Spain, but he came into the world just seven years before the Christian rulers Ferdinand and Isabella drove out all Muslims in 1492. Therefore he and his family fled to Morocco, where his uncle became an official in the Islamic government. Thus the young man had an opportunity to travel throughout northern Africa, but on one trip in 1517, when he was thirty-two years old, he was captured and enslaved by European pirates.

Up to this point, he had been known by an Arabic name, but when his reputation as an extremely learned slave gained him an introduction to Pope Leo X (ruled 1513–21), the pope took such a liking to him that he gave him his own name. Thus he became Leo Africanus, or Leo the African, and accepted Christianity. Under the pope's direction, he wrote *Description of Africa,* which for many years remained Europeans' primary source of knowledge on Africa.

would come to an end in just a few years; but behind the scenes, a clash of cultures was forming. The capital of Ghana, Kumbi-Saleh, had been formed from two towns about six miles apart. One town became a center for Islam, al-Bekri's own religion, whereas the other remained a stronghold of the native religion. Eventually the Muslim faith would win out, in the process destroying the power of the king, whose people had believed he was a god.

Timbuktu, on the other hand, was predominantly Muslim when Leo Africanus, another Islamic traveler, visited there. (His reference to the ruler's dislike for Jews, however, is not typical of medieval Islam: during the Middle Ages, Jews and Muslims typically got along well.) Yet Timbuktu faced other threats. One of these was the harsh surrounding environment, to which Leo referred in his account. Another was the near-constant state of warfare between various African peoples in the area. Though they were not necessarily of different races, their cultures and ways of life were often in conflict, and eventually this struggle would bring an end to the glory of Timbuktu.

Things to remember while reading the excerpts from *Al-Masalik wa 'l-Mamalik* and *Description of Africa*

- Though the term "Negro" came to have a negative meaning in the late twentieth century, al-Bekri's use of it does not imply a racial judgment; rather, he used it as a simple descriptive term equivalent to the word "Caucasian" for white people.

- Both writers were born in Spain when it was under Islamic control, but Leo Africanus wrote his account for Europeans. Therefore he used units of measure such as the mile and the *ducat* (DUK-et), a type of money in Europe, whereas al-Bekri used Middle Eastern words: *dinar* (dee-NAHR) and *mitqal* (meet-KAHL) for units of money, and *vizier* (VIZ-ee-ur) for a type of government official.

Fihini Village in modern-day Ghana. When al-Bekri visited Ghana in about 1067, the empire was extremely wealthy and powerful. *Reproduced by permission of the Corbis Corporation.*

- The two writers make a number of interesting observations about the economic systems of Ghana and Timbuktu. Salt was and is a highly valued item in the Sahara: even today, African merchants do a brisk business selling the mineral, which is necessary to human life but scarce in the region. Al-Bekri also noted that if the king of Ghana did not control the supply of gold, it would lose its worth, a fact that is true of any unit of value, whether it be gold, paper money, or another item. Leo Africanus, for his part, perhaps said a great deal when he wrote that "The inhabitants are very rich, especially the strangers who have settled in the country." This seems to imply that the people of Timbuktu

were not becoming wealthy in as great numbers as the foreigners in their midst.

• Many of the names used by the two travelers are lost to history. The locations of Ghiaru and Tegaza are not clear. Nor is there much information about the architect named Granata, who must surely have been a prominent citizen of Timbuktu.

Excerpt from Al-Masalik wa 'l-Mamalik

The king of Ghana can put two hundred thousand warriors in the field, more than forty thousand being armed with bow and arrow....

*When he gives **audience** to his people, to listen to their complaints and set them to rights, he sits in a **pavilion** around which stand ten pages holding shields and gold-mounted swords: and on his right hand are the sons of the princes of his empire, splendidly clad and with gold plaited into their hair. The governor of the city is seated on the ground in front of the king, and all around him are his **vizirs** in the same position. The gate of the chamber is guarded by dogs of an excellent breed, who never leave the king's seat: they wear collars of gold and silver, ornamented with the same metals. The beginning of a royal audience is announced by the beating of a kind of drum which they call deba, made of a long piece of hollowed wood. The people gather when they hear this sound....*

*The king exacts the right of one **dinar** of gold on each donkey-load of salt that enters his country, and two dinars of gold on each load of salt that goes out. A load of copper carries a **duty** of five **mitqals** and a load of merchandise ten mitqals. The best gold in the country comes from Ghiaru, a town situated eighteen days' journey from the capital in a country that is densely populated by Negroes and covered with villages. All pieces of native gold found in the mines of the empire belong to the **sovereign**, although he lets the public have the gold dust that everybody knows about; without this precaution, gold would become so abundant as practically to lose its value....*

Excerpt from Description of Africa

*The houses of Timbuktu are huts made of clay-covered **wattles** with thatched roofs. In the center of the city is a temple built of stone and mortar, built by an architect named Granata, and in addition there is a large palace, constructed by the same architect, where the king lives. The shops of the **artisans**, the merchants, and especially weavers of cotton cloth are very numerous. Fabrics are also imported from Europe to Timbuktu, borne by **Berber** merchants.*

Audience: A ruler's formal review of his people's concerns.

Pavilion: A covered area open on the sides.

Vizirs (or viziers): High government officials in Middle Eastern and some African lands.

Dinar: A type of gold coin used in the Middle East and North Africa at one time.

Duty: Tax.

Mitqal: A unit of money in some Middle Eastern and African regions.

Sovereign: King.

Wattles: A group of poles woven together with reeds or branches to form a structure.

Artisans: Skilled workers who produce items according to their specialty.

Berber: A general term describing several groups of people in northwestern Africa.

The women of the city maintain the custom of veiling their faces, except for the slaves who sell all the foodstuffs. The inhabitants are very rich, especially the strangers who have settled in the country; so much so that the current king has given two of his daughters in marriage to two brothers, both businessmen, on account of their wealth. There are many wells containing **sweet water** in Timbuktu.... Grain and animals are abundant, so that the consumption of milk and butter is considerable. But salt is in very short supply because it is carried here from Tegaza, some 500 miles from Timbuktu. I happened to be in this city at a time when a load of salt sold for eighty **ducats**. The king has a rich treasure of coins and gold ingots. One of these **ingots** weighs 970 pounds.

The royal court is magnificent and very well organized. When the king goes from one city to another with the people of his court, he rides a camel and the horses are led by hand by servants. If fighting becomes necessary, the servants mount the camels and all the soldiers mount on horseback. When someone wishes to speak to the king, he must kneel before him and bow down; but this is only required of those who have never before spoken to the king, or of ambassadors [from other countries]. The king has about 3,000 horsemen and **infinity** of foot-soldiers armed with bows ... which they use to shoot poisoned arrows. This king makes war only upon neighboring enemies and upon those who do not want to pay him **tribute**. When he has gained a victory, he has all of them—even the children—sold in the market at Timbuktu.

Only small, poor horses are born in this country. The merchants use them for their voyages and the courtiers to move about the city. But the good horses come from **Barbary**. They arrive in a caravan and, ten or twelve days later, they are led to the ruler, who takes as many as he likes and pays appropriately for them.

The king is a declared enemy of the Jews. He will not allow any to live in the city. If he hears it said that a Berber merchant frequents them or does business with them, he **confiscates** his goods. There are in Timbuktu numerous judges, teachers and priests, all properly appointed by the king. He greatly honors learning. Many handwritten books imported from Barbary are also sold. There is more profit made from this commerce than from all other merchandise.

Instead of coined money, pure gold nuggets are used; and for small purchases, **cowrie shells**, which have been carried from Persia, and of which 400 equal a ducat. Six and two-thirds of their ducats equal one Roman gold ounce.

Sweet water: Drinkable water.

Ducats: A type of coin used in medieval and Renaissance Europe.

Ingots: Blocks of gold or other metals.

Infinity: Literally, an unlimited number; in this case, however, a very large number.

Tribute: Forced payments to a king or conqueror.

Barbary: A term used in premodern times to refer to the Mediterranean coast of North Africa.

Confiscates: Seizes.

Cowrie shells: Bright shells that come from a variety of ocean creatures, used as money in some countries before modern times.

The people of Timbuktu are of a peaceful nature. They have a custom of almost continuously walking about the city in the evening (except for those that sell gold), between 10 P.M. and 1 A.M., playing musical instruments and dancing. The citizens have at their service many slaves, both men and women.

The city is very much endangered by fire. At the time when I was there on my second voyage, half the city burned in the space of five hours. But the wind was violent and the inhabitants of the other half of the city began to move their belongings for fear that the other half would burn.

There are no gardens or orchards in the area surrounding Timbuktu.

Modern-day Timbuktu, in the nation of Mali, shows little sign of the wealth described by Leo Africanus from his visit to the empire of Mali in the sixteenth century. *Reproduced by permission of the Corbis Corporation.*

What happened next ...

In 1080, just thirteen years after al-Bekri's visit, Ghana suffered an invasion by Muslim conquerors from Morocco in the north. Despite its wealth and the apparent power of its king—power which had already been weakened by the people's acceptance of a religion from outside—the empire of Ghana quickly disappeared.

Within the next two centuries, a new empire arose in Mali, and from the 1200s, it came to dominate the region. Despite the strong leadership of several kings, however, Mali was also overtaken—this time by invaders from within the region. The new power, Songhai, oversaw Timbuktu at its height, a period that actually preceded the visit of Leo Africanus. Yet like the empire of Ghana five centuries before, Songhai fell to conquerors from Morocco in 1591.

Because of Leo Africanus, Timbuktu remained alive in the imagination of Europeans, yet it would be three centuries before another outsider visited the region and wrote about it, and in the meantime it suffered a series of wars and invasions. In 1828, a French explorer went to find the legendary city, and in its place he found a "mass of ill-looking houses built of earth." Eventually, the name "Timbuktu" became a synonym for a remote, forgotten place.

Did you know ...

- The emperor of Ghana was not the only ruler in the region noted for his great wealth in gold; another was Mansa Musa (ruled 1307–c. 1332), who reigned at the height of Mali's power and became the first African ruler to become widely known throughout Europe and the Middle East. He once made a visit to Egypt, where he spent so much that he actually caused an oversupply of gold (and resulting economic problems) in that country.

- Today there is an African country called Ghana, but it is actually located in an area to the south of the former empire by that name. The nation of Mauritania contains most of what was called Ghana in premodern times. There is also a country called Mali, but its boundaries are not the same as the lands once controlled by the empire of Mali. The nation of Mali does, however, contain Timbuktu—or rather, Tombouctou (tohn-buk-TOO), a town of some 30,000 inhabitants.

For More Information

Books

Brians, Paul, et al., editors. *Readings about the World, Volume 2*. New York: Harcourt Brace Custom Books, 1999.

Davidson, Basil. *African Kingdoms*. Alexandria, VA: Time-Life Books, 1978.

Davidson, Basil, editor. *African Civilization Revisited*. Trenton, NJ: Africa World Press, 1991.

McKissack, Pat. *The Royal Kingdoms of Ghana, Mali, and Songhay: Life in Medieval Africa*. New York: Henry Holt, 1994.

Web Sites

"African Empires Timeline." [Online] Available http://www.cocc.edu/cagatucci/classes/hum211/timelines/htimeline2.htm (last accessed July 28, 2000).

"Glimpses of the Kingdom of Ghana in 1067 CE." [Online] Available http://www.humanities.ccny.cuny.edu/history/reader/ghana.htm (last accessed July 28, 2000).

Marco Polo

Excerpt from **The Book of Ser Marco Polo the Venetian Concerning the Kingdoms and Marvels of the East**
Published in 1903

The Mongols were a nomadic, or wandering, people who lived in Central Asia between China and what is now Russia—the area of modern-day Mongolia. For a brief period during the 1200s, this small nation of warriors controlled much of the known world, thanks to a series of conquests begun by Genghis Khan (JING-us KAHN; c. 1162–1227). Under his leadership and that of those who followed, the Mongols took control of an area that stretched from the Korean Peninsula to the outskirts of Vienna, Austria, a distance of about 4,500 miles.

After Genghis, the greatest Mongol khan, or ruler, was Kublai Khan (KOO-bluh; 1215–1294; ruled 1260–1294), who led the Mongols in the conquest of China. For centuries, the Chinese had regarded the Mongols and other nomadic tribes with distrust, and they regarded Kublai's victory over them in 1279 as a disaster. Yet the short-lived Mongol empire also had the effect of opening up trade routes, and as a result there was more contact between East and West than ever before.

This situation made possible one of the most celebrated journeys in history, by Marco Polo (1254–1324) and his father and uncle. Marco won such great favor with Kublai Khan

"I repeat that everything appertaining to this city is on so vast a scale, and the Great Kaan's yearly revenues therefrom are so immense, that it is not easy even to put it in writing, and it seems past belief to one who merely hears it told."

Marco Polo

In 1271, when he was seventeen years old, Marco Polo set out from his hometown of Venice, Italy, with his father and uncle. Today one can fly from Venice to China in just a few hours; but the Polos' journey—which took them through Persia, Afghanistan, northern India, and into China—lasted three years. Along the way, Marco learned several languages, skills that would help them when they got to their destination.

China at that time was under the control of the Mongols, a nomadic tribe from Central Asia, and the Mongol emperor Kublai Khan was perhaps the most powerful man on Earth. Marco became a minister in the Khan's government, which gave him the opportunity to travel throughout southeastern Asia in the coming years.

By 1287, however, when Marco was thirty-three years old, his aging father and uncle were ready to return home. It took some time to obtain the Khan's approval for them to leave, and the return journey by ship was every bit as difficult as the trip out had been; but finally, in 1295, they returned to Venice.

Marco Polo. *Reproduced by permission of the Library of Congress.*

In 1298, during a war with the rival Italian city of Genoa (JIN-oh-uh), Marco was captured and thrown into a Genoese prison. There he met a writer named Rustichello, to whom he told the story of his travels, and Rustichello began writing a book that would become known in English as *The Book of Ser Marco Polo*. The book would later be recognized as the basis for scientific geography, and greatly expanded Europeans' understanding of the world.

that the ruler made him a trusted official in his government, and as a result he had an opportunity to travel to lands that no European had ever seen. Marco marveled at the wonders of the Mongols' government, and at the highly advanced civilization of the Chinese they had conquered. Later, when he returned to his hometown of Venice, Italy, he recorded these and other observations in a work the English title of which became *The Book of Ser Marco Polo the Venetian Concerning the Kingdoms and Marvels of the East.* (*Ser* is an abbreviation of the Italian term for "mister.")

Things to remember while reading the excerpt from *The Book of Ser Marco Polo the Venetian*

- The passage that follows contains Marco Polo's description of a city in eastern China that he called Kinsay (kin-SY), but which is known today as Hangzhou (hahng-ZHOH). That city had been the capital of China prior to the Mongol conquest. He also used the term Manzi (mahn-ZEE) to describe southern China, and Cathay (kah-THY) for China as a whole. As for the port he described at Ganfu (gahn-FOO), that city has since been covered by ocean. Marco's use of the term "Ocean Sea" reflects a pre-modern European belief that all the world's land was surrounded by a single body of water.

- When Marco referred to "miles," he was probably using a Chinese unit called a *li* (LEE), equal to about two-fifths of a mile. He also used an alternative spelling of *khan,* kaan. Other spellings in this document, such as *armour* or *honour,* however, are not necessarily Marco's but those of the translator, who was British. This also explains the use of the British term *burgess* for "citizen."

- Europeans during the Middle Ages did not bathe on a regular basis, thinking it was unhealthy to do so; but Marco could not help being impressed—understandably so—by the cleanliness of the Chinese. In the latter part of this passage, he reveals the ill-will of the Chinese toward their Mongol conquerors, who they regarded both as outsiders and as barbarians, or uncivilized people; yet to judge from this account at least, they did not seem to treat Marco with similar scorn.

- One fact that makes Marco's history of his journeys so entertaining is that he was more open-minded than most Europeans of his time; one would have to be to travel so far from home. Yet it was sometimes hard to keep his prejudices from showing through, as for instance when he referred to the Chinese as idol-worshipers. In fact the people of China subscribed to a number of religions, few of which could be considered any more idolatrous than the worship of saints practiced by European Christians at the time.

Excerpt from The Book of Ser Marco Polo the Venetian Concerning the Kingdoms and Marvels of the East

You must know also that the city of Kinsay has some 3,000 baths, the water of which is supplied by springs. They are hot baths, and the people take great delight in them, frequenting them several times a month, for they are very cleanly in their persons. They are the finest and largest baths in the world; large enough for 100 persons to bathe together.

*And the Ocean Sea comes within 25 miles of the city at a place called Ganfu, where there is a town and an excellent **haven**, with a vast amount of shipping which is engaged in the traffic to and from India and other foreign parts, exporting and importing many kinds of wares, by which the city benefits. And a great river flows from the city of Kinsay to that sea-haven, by which vessels can come up to the city itself. This river extends also to other places further inland....*

*I repeat that everything **appertaining** to this city is on so vast a scale, and the Great Kaan's yearly revenues therefrom are so immense, that it is not easy even to put it in writing, and it seems past belief to one who merely hears it told. But I will write it down for you.*

*First, however, I must mention another thing. The people of this country have a custom, that as soon as a child is born they write down the day and hour and the planet and sign under which its birth has taken place; so that every one among them knows the day of his birth. And when any one intends a journey he goes to the **astrologers** and gives the particulars of his nativity in order to learn whether he shall have good luck or no. Sometimes they will say no, and in that case the journey is put off till such day as the astrologer may recommend. These astrologers are very skillful at their business, and often their words come to pass, so the people have great faith in them.*

Haven: Harbor.

Appertaining: Pertaining, or with regard to.

Astrologers: People who study the stars and planets with the belief that their movement has an effect on personal events.

*They burn the bodies of the dead. And when any one dies the friends and relations make a great mourning for the deceased, and clothe themselves in hempen garments, and follow the corpse playing on a variety of instruments and singing hymns to their idols. And when they come to the burning place, they take representations of things cut out of parchment, such as **caparisoned** horses, male and female slaves, camels, armour, suits of cloth or gold (and money), in great quantities, and these things they put on the fire along with the corpse, so that they are all burnt with it. And they tell you that the dead man shall have all these slaves and animals of which the effigies are burnt, alive in flesh and blood, and the money in gold, at his disposal in the next world; and that the instruments which they have caused to be played at his funeral, and the idol hymns that have been chanted, shall also be produced again to welcome him in the next world; and that the idols themselves will come to do him honour....*

*There is another thing I must tell you. It is the custom for every **burgess** of this city, and in fact for every description of person in it,*

Marco Polo kneels before Kublai Khan. *Reproduced by permission of the Corbis Corporation.*

Caparisoned: Equipped with a decorative covering.

Burgess: Citizen.

Was Marco Polo Telling the Truth?

The journeys of Marco Polo were as remarkable in the Middle Ages as travel to another planet would be in modern times, and the information he brought back to Europe greatly expanded human knowledge. But his stories about faraway lands sounded so outrageous, and involved so many big numbers, that his neighbors nicknamed him "Marco Millions."

Some modern scholars have been similarly inclined to disbelieve Marco's tales. For instance, they point out that many of the words he used were in Farsi, the language of Persia, which would imply that he never actually went any farther east than modern-day Iran. But Farsi was the language of international trade at that time, much as English is today, so it is understandable that educated local people would have conversed with Marco in that language.

Harder to explain is the fact that Marco failed to mention either the Great Wall of China or the practice of foot-binding, or wrapping a young girl's feet in strips of cloth to prevent them from growing. This caused a grown woman to have tiny feet, something the Chinese at the time considered the height of beauty, but something a European would have found shocking. As for the Great Wall, his route should have taken him near it, and with its enormous size, it is hard to miss.

On the other hand, Marco certainly would have known about the Great Wall, which had been built in the 200s B.C. Therefore if he had been falsifying his account, he would have had every reason to mention it as a way of making his record seem more accurate. As for foot-binding, because this was a Chinese and not a Mongol practice—and because Marco was associated with the Mongols, who were foreigners in the view of the Chinese—perhaps he did not become intimately acquainted enough with the Chinese to learn about this practice.

Inmates: Inhabitants or residents.

Sovereign: Ruler.

Hosteler: Innkeeper or hotel manager.

Surnames: Family names—in European-influenced cultures, the last name, but in China the first name.

to write over his door his own name, the name of his wife, and those of his children, his slaves, and all the **inmates** of his house, and also the number of animals that he keeps. And if any one dies in the house then the name of that person is erased, and if any child is born its name is added. So in this way the **sovereign** is able to know exactly the population of the city. And this is the practice also throughout all Manzi and Cathay.

And I must tell you that every **hosteler** who keeps an hostel for travellers is bound to register their names and **surnames**, as well as the day and month of their arrival and departure. And thus the sov-

ereign hath the means of knowing, whenever it pleases him, who come and go throughout his dominions....

*Other streets are occupied by the Physicians, and by the Astrologers, who are also teachers of reading and writing; and an infinity of other professions have their places round about those squares. In each of the squares there are two great palaces facing one another, in which are established the officers appointed by the King to decide differences arising between merchants, or other inhabitants of the quarter. It is the daily duty of these officers to see that the guards are at their posts on the neighbouring bridges, and to punish them at their **discretion** if they are absent....*

The natives of the city are men of peaceful character, both from education and from the example of their kings, whose disposition was the same. They know nothing of handling arms, and keep none in their houses. You hear of no feuds or noisy quarrels or dissensions of any kind among them. Both in their commercial dealings and in their manufactures they are thoroughly honest and truthful, and there is such a degree of good will and neighbourly attachment among both men and women that you would take the people who live in the same street to be all one family.

*And this familiar intimacy is free from all jealousy or suspicion of the conduct of their women. These they treat with the greatest respect, and a man who should presume to make loose proposals to a married woman would be regarded as an infamous rascal. They also treat the foreigners who visit them for the sake of trade with great **cordiality,** and entertain them in the most winning manner, affording them every help and advice on their business. But on the other hand they hate to see soldiers, and not least those of the Great Kaan's garrisons, regarding them as the cause of their having lost their native kings and lords....*

Discretion: Judgment.

Cordiality: Courtesy.

What happened next ...

As it turned out, Marco Polo had seen China during the height of the Mongols' power. Already in 1274 and 1281, Kublai Khan had shown that his forces could be defeated when he launched two failed invasions of Japan; and in 1293

Kublai Khan was one of the most powerful men on Earth when Marco Polo traveled to China in the 1270s.
Reproduced by permission of the Library of Congress.

he suffered another defeat in trying to take the island of Java in what is now Indonesia. Kublai died in the following year, and the Mongol dynasty rapidly declined thereafter. In 1368, the Chinese overthrew it and established the Ming dynasty, which would rule until 1644.

Marco's account of his travels, which he began while in prison in 1298, became one of the most important works of geography ever written. It provided Europeans with their first exposure to many lands and peoples of the East, and increased their interest in learning more. As this interest grew, it led to expeditions and voyages of exploration that in turn advanced Europeans' knowledge even more. The Chinese, by contrast, had little interest in learning about people outside their realms. Though they sent ships to far-flung regions in the early 1400s, the purpose of these voyages was not exploration or even conquest; rather, it was to display Chinese achievements. While China turned inward, Europeans' thirst for knowledge ultimately gave them an advantage over the civilization that had created printing, firearms, and many other inventions that would change the world.

One reader later inspired by Marco's account was a fellow Italian named Christopher Columbus (1451–1506). Coincidentally, Columbus came from Genoa, a rival city of Venice that had imprisoned Marco and thus indirectly influenced him to write about his travels. In 1492, as every student knows, Columbus set out to reach China by a sea route, but found the New World instead.

Did you know ...
• Marco Polo's book provided Europeans with their first knowledge of the Pamir (puh-MEER) range between

Afghanistan and China. The Pamirs are among the world's highest mountains, and while there, Marco saw an animal that was later named the "Marco Polo sheep" in his honor.

• During Marco's lifetime, Kublai Khan sent a journeyer westward: Rabban Bar Sauma (ruh-BAHN BAR sah-OO-muh; c. 1220–1294). Born in China, Bar Sauma was a Turkish monk of the Nestorian faith, a breakaway group of Christians. In Europe, he met with the pope, and the two joined in an unsuccessful attempt to raise a crusade or "holy war" against the Muslims in the Middle East.

For More Information

Books

MacDonald, Fiona. *Marco Polo: A Journey through China.* Illustrated by Mark Bergin, created and designed by David Salariya. New York: Franklin Watts, 1998.

Polo, Marco. *The Book of Ser Marco Polo the Venetian Concerning the Kingdoms and Marvels of the East.* Translated and edited by Henry Yule, third edition revised by Henri Cordier. London: John Murray, 1903.

Roth, Susan L. *Marco Polo: His Notebook.* New York: Doubleday, 1990.

Web Sites

"Marco Polo and His Travels." *Silkroad Foundation.* [Online] Available http://www.silk-road.com/artl/marcopolo.shtml (last accessed July 28, 2000).

Marco Polo: His Travels and Their Effects on the World. [Online] Available http://www.geocities.com/TimesSquare/Maze/5099/sld001.html (last accessed July 28, 2000).

"Medieval Sourcebook: Marco Polo: The Glories of Kinsay [Hangchow] (c. 1300)." *Medieval Sourcebook.* [Online] Available http://www.fordham.edu/halsall/source/polo-kinsay.html (last accessed July 28, 2000).

Jacob von Königshofen

"The Cremation of Strasbourg Jewry,
St. Valentine's Day, February 14, 1349—
About the Great Plague and the Burning of the Jews"
Published in *The Jew in the Medieval World*, 1938

Between 1347 and 1351, Europe suffered one of the worst disasters of human history: the Black Death, sometimes known simply as the Plague. A disease carried by bacteria, or microscopic organisms, the Plague spread rapidly throughout the continent, killing between twenty-five and thirty-five million people out of a population estimated at 100 million. Victims usually died within four days of contracting the disease, but they were four days of horror. In the final hours, the victim turned purplish-black from lung failure; hence the name Black Death.

The medical causes of the Black Death are clear today, but medieval Europeans had no concept of bacteria. Instead, some blamed spiritual causes, while others found a different target: the Jews. For many years, a spirit of anti-Semitism (hatred of, or discrimination against, Jews) had been brewing in Europe, and many justified this hatred in religious terms, saying that the Jews had killed Christ.

As a result, Jews were forced into the fringes of society, and were only allowed to engage in certain jobs such as money-lending, which at that time was considered an evil

> "The deputies of the city of Strasbourg were asked what they were going to do with their Jews. They answered and said that they knew no evil of them. Then they asked the Strasbourgers why they had closed the wells and put away the buckets, and there was a great indignation and clamor against the deputies from Strasbourg."

Jewish Sympathizers—A Rare Breed

Jacob von Königshofen is a little-known figure, but perhaps he should not be. He served as town historian for Strasbourg, a German-speaking city that is now just inside the French border, and he was a rare type in medieval Western Europe: a Christian who had sympathy for the Jews.

Jews were all too often the target of attacks from the 1000s onward, and this reached a new low during the Black Death, a massive outbreak of disease that killed between twenty-five and thirty-five million Europeans between 1347 and 1351. Desperate for someone to blame, many Europeans were all too willing to believe that Jews had poisoned wells, thus causing the disease.

From his account, it is clear that Königshofen considered the Jews victims, and not the cause of anyone's misfortune. This was a brave stance in a world where Jews were safe targets. Also brave were the city councilmen to whom he referred, men who stood up against the mobs calling for Jewish blood.

Finally, it is interesting to observe that Pope Clement VI (ruled 1342–52), along with other leaders of the Catholic Church, defended the Jews: some Church leaders have openly condemned people of the Jewish faith for what they believe to be the Jews' role in the death of Jesus Christ. In fact the Roman authorities of Palestine at the time of the crucifixion had much to do with Jesus' murder, and most Christians believe that all of humanity—not one group of people—was responsible for Christ's death. But most Christians in the Middle Ages did not believe this, or at least they were afraid to say so in the feverish climate of hatred directed against the Jewish people, and this makes the stance of Königshofen and the others all the more remarkable.

profession. This created a vicious cycle: their financial undertakings made many Jews wealthy, and Europeans increasingly came to despise them for their wealth as well.

Anti-Semitism first boiled over during the First Crusade (1095–99), when European armies seized Palestine—the Jews' original homeland—from the Muslims who controlled it. Many other Europeans, too poor to go away and fight, decided they could still wage war on people who had rejected Christ, so they launched a series of attacks on the Jews in Europe. Some 150 years later, the Black Death provided an excuse for a whole new wave of anti-Semitism.

A Jewish synagogue. The Black Death prompted intense hatred and persecution of Jews as many Europeans looked for someone to blame for the disease. *Reproduced by permission of the Corbis Corporation.*

Things to remember while reading "The Cremation of Strasbourg Jewry, St. Valentine's Day, February 14, 1349"

- Jacob von Königshofen (KYOO-nigs-hahf-en; 1346–1420) served as town historian for Strasbourg (STRAHS-boorg), a German-speaking city in what is now France. Alsace (al-SAS), also mentioned in his account, is a region on the border between France and Germany. His chronicle refers to a number of Swiss cities: Berne, Zofingen (TSOH-fing-en), and Basel (BAHL). These he calls "Imperial Cities" because they were part of the Holy Roman Empire, a collection of states based in what is now Germany. He also mentions the southern French cities of Marseilles (mar-SAY) and Avignon (AHV-in-yawn). Since 1309, the popes had ruled from the latter city rather than from their traditional seat in Rome.

- The term "Jewry" refers to Jews as a whole, and from his account, it is clear that Königshofen did not believe the accusations leveled against them. He even observed that many were killed simply for their money. When he wrote that some Jews had "admitted" to poisoning wells, he was referring to false "confessions" that had been extracted after hours of torture.

- The separation of Jews from Christians in medieval Europe continued after death; hence Königshofen referred to the Jews having their own cemetery. He also noted that some Jews escaped death by accepting baptism, a ritual that supposedly meant that they had converted to Christianity—though given the circumstances, it is hard to imagine that any of these conversions were genuine. It is interesting to note that the massacre described took place on the day honoring the patron saint of love, Valentine.

- There are several references to fire in Königshofen's report—in most cases, the fires in which Jews died. A well-known method of execution during the Middle Ages was burning at the stake, in which a victim was bound to a pole and heaped with branches around their feet; the branches were then set on fire, burning the victim alive. But Königshofen also noted that the pope kept a fire burning in a room, probably intending this as a way of disinfecting the air and thus keeping the Plague away from him.

- Königshofen describes a conference attended by the deputies or city councilmen of several cities, who met to decide the fate of Jews arrested in their various jurisdictions. The Strasbourg deputies, at least, were prepared to free those who had been arrested, and defiantly demanded to know why the citizens of their town had closed all wells—suggesting that they did not believe the popular claim that the Plague had resulted from Jews' poisoning of the water supply. Unfortunately, it is clear from the text that the heroic Strasbourg deputies were overruled.

"The Cremation of Strasbourg Jewry St. Valentine's Day, February 14, 1349—About the Great Plague and the Burning of the Jews"

*In the year 1349 there occurred the greatest **epidemic** that ever happened. Death went from one end of the earth to the other, on that side and this side of the sea.... In some lands everyone died so that no one was left. Ships were also found on the sea laden with **wares**; the crew had all died and no one guided the ship. The Bishop of Marseilles and priests and monks and more than half of all the people there died with them. In other kingdoms and cities so many people perished that it would be horrible to describe. The pope at Avignon stopped all sessions of court, locked himself in a room, allowed no one to approach him and had a fire burning before him all the time. And from what this epidemic came, all wise teachers and physicians could only say that it was God's will. And as the **plague** was now here, so was it in other places, and lasted more than a whole year. This epidemic also came to Strasbourg in the summer of the above mentioned year, and it is estimated that about sixteen thousand people died.*

*In the matter of this plague the Jews throughout the world were **reviled** and accused in all lands of having caused it through the poison which they are said to have put into the water and the wells— that is what they were accused of—and for this reason the Jews were burnt all the way from the Mediterranean into Germany, but not in Avignon, for the pope protected them there.*

Nevertheless they tortured a number of Jews in Berne and Zofingen who then admitted that they had put poison into many wells, and they also found the poison in the wells. Thereupon they burnt the Jews in many towns and wrote of this affair to Strasbourg, Freiburg, and Basel in order that they too should burn their Jews. But the leaders in these three cities in whose hands the government lay did not believe that anything ought to be done to the Jews. However

Epidemic: A widespread disease.

Wares: Cargo.

Plague: A disease or other bad thing that spreads among a group of people.

Reviled: Despised.

*in Basel the citizens marched to the city-hall and compelled the council to take an oath that they would burn the Jews, and that they would allow no Jew to enter the city for the next two hundred years. Thereupon the Jews were arrested in all these places and a conference was arranged to meet [in] ... Alsace, February 8, 1349. The **Bishop** of Strasbourg, all the **feudal lords** of Alsace, and representatives of the three above mentioned cities came there. The **deputies** of the city of Strasbourg were asked what they were going to do with their Jews. They answered and said that they knew no evil of them. Then they [the deputies] asked the Strasbourgers why they had closed the wells and put away the buckets, and there was a great **indignation** and **clamor** against the deputies from Strasbourg. So finally the Bishop and the lords and the Imperial Cities agreed to do away with the Jews. The result was that they were burnt in many cities, and wherever they were expelled they were caught by the peasants and stabbed to death or drowned....*

The Jews Are Burnt

*On Saturday—that was St. Valentine's Day—they burnt the Jews on a wooden platform in their cemetery. There were about two thousand people of them. Those who wanted to **baptize** themselves were spared. Many small children were taken out of the fire and baptized against the will of their fathers and mothers. And everything that was owed to the Jews was cancelled, and the Jews had to surrender all pledges and notes that they had taken for debts. The council, however, took the cash that the Jews possessed and divided it among the working-men **proportionately**. The money was indeed the thing that killed the Jews. If they had been poor and if the feudal lords had not been in debt to them, they would not have been burnt. After this wealth was divided among the artisans some gave their share to the Cathedral or to the Church on the advice of their confessors.*

*Thus were the Jews burnt at Strasbourg, and in the same year in all the cities of the Rhine, whether Free Cities or Imperial Cities or cities belonging to the lords. In some towns they burnt the Jews after a trial, in others, without a trial. In some cities the Jews themselves set fire to their houses and **cremated** themselves.*

Bishop: A figure in the Christian church assigned to oversee priests and believers in a given city or region.

Feudal lords: Nobility or large landowners.

Deputies: City councilmen.

Indignation: Irritation or anger.

Clamor: Loud noise.

Baptize: Lowered into water as a symbol of death and rebirth; considered by some to be a necessary part of conversion to Christianity.

Proportionately: Evenly.

Cremated: Burned completely.

The text within the image reads:

Der Doctor Schna- -bel von Rom

Vos Creditis, als eine fabel.
quod scribitur von Doctor schnabel.
der fugit die Contagion
et auffert seinen Lohn darvon.
Cadavera sucht er zu fristen
gleich wie der Corvus auf der Misten.
Ah Credite, ziht nicht dort hin
dann Romæ regnat die Pestin.

Quis non deberet sehr erschrec
für seiner Virgul oder stecken.
quâ loquitur. als wär er stumm.
und deütet sein consilium.
Wie mancher Credit ohne zweiffel
das ihm tentir ein schwarzen Teüffl
Marsupium heyst seine Höll.
und aurum die geholte seel

I. Columbina, ad vivum delineavt   Paulus Fürst Excud:

Kleidung wider den Tod zu Rom. Anno 1656.
Also gehen die Doctores Medici daheÿ zu Rom, wann sie die, an der Pest erkrancket Personen besuchen, sie zu curiren und fragen, sich wider den Gifft zu sichern, ein langes Kleid von gewärtem Tuch ihr Angesicht ist verlarvt, für den Augen haben sie grosse Crÿstalline Brillen, wider Nasen einen langen Schnabel voll wolriechender Specereÿ, in der Hände, welche mit Handschuhen wolversehen ist, eine lange Rüthe, und darmit däuten sie, was man thun, und gebrauchē soll

Abb. 63. Pestarzt in einer Schutzkleidung. Kpfr. von Paulus Fürst nach
J. Columbina 1656. München, Kupferstichkabinet.

The protective clothing of a physician treating people with the Plague. The Plague, or Black Death, killed between twenty-five and thirty-five million people in Europe in the mid-1300s. *Reproduced by permission of the Corbis Corporation.*

What happened next...

Königshofen wrote, "It was decided in Strasbourg that no Jew should enter the city for a hundred years, but before twenty years had passed, the council and magistrates agreed that they ought to admit the Jews again into the city for twenty years. And so the Jews came back again to Strasbourg in the year 1368...."

Jewish life in Germany, however, did not fully recover until three centuries later, in the 1600s. Then, three centuries after that, European Jews suffered the worst wave of anti-Semitic murders in history, under the Nazi government of Adolf Hitler: during the years from 1933 to 1945, some six million Jews were killed by the Nazis.

Europe's recovery from the Black Death was much quicker than that of the Jewish population, though still quite painful. The disease had left so many people dead that the population did not return to its earlier levels until about 1500, and the economic loss that resulted from the deaths brought on more hardship and unrest.

Did you know ...

- The Strasbourg town councilmen who stood up against the mob calling for Jewish blood were removed from office on February 9 and 10, 1349. A new city council agreed to the demands of their citizens, and began arresting Jews on February 13, the day before the massacre described by Königshofen.

- If a tragedy on the scale of the Black Death occurred in America today, it would be the same as if all the people in the six most populous states—California, New York, Texas, Florida, Pennsylvania, and Illinois—died over a four-year period.

- The Black Death, combined with the struggle between forces who wanted the popes to rule from Rome and those who favored Avignon, helped bring about a massive loss of faith in the Catholic Church. This in turn paved the way for the Reformation (ref-ur-MAY-shun), the religious revolt that began in the 1300s that later created the Protestant branch of Christianity.

For More Information

Books

Abrahams, Israel. *Jewish Life in the Middle Ages.* Philadelphia: Jewish Publication Society, 1993.

Marcus, Jacob, editor. *The Jew in the Medieval World: A Sourcebook, 315–1791.* New York: JPS, 1938.

Web Sites

"Beyond the Pale: The Middle Ages." [Online] Available http://www.friends-partners.org/partners/beyond-the-pale/english/06.html (last accessed July 28, 2000).

"Jewish History Sourcebook: The Black Death and the Jews 1348–1349 CE." *Jewish History Sourcebook.* [Online] Available http://www.fordham.edu/halsall/jewish/1348-jewsblackdeath.html (last accessed July 28, 2000).

Personal Life

People in the modern West—that is, Europe and the countries influenced by European civilization—tend to hold certain views on human personality and feelings. Typically, Westerners place a high emphasis on the individual: each person is unique and special, they would say, with a right to choose their own destiny. Yet as obvious as this viewpoint might seem to most Americans, it is far from universal. In many parts of the world today, people hold a strikingly different view of the individual: in several non-Western societies, submission to parents, teachers, and rulers is encouraged while self-interest or individual expression is discouraged. Nor has the West always been so oriented toward the self or the individual; these concepts have only come to the forefront of Western thinking in recent centuries.

In part for this reason, the *Confessions* of **Augustine** (aw-GUS-tin; 354–430) is considered one of the greatest works of Western literature. Here, in a work so old it almost qualifies as ancient rather than medieval, is a view of the self—including inner struggles of right and wrong within the soul—familiar to modern readers. This is all the more remarkable when one considers the few deeply personal writings that preceded it, and the even fewer ones that followed it for a thousand years. Outside of certain passages in the Bible, it is hard to find ancient literature that asks probing personal questions, or that expresses feelings from the bottom of the heart; nor would such intensely introspective (inward-looking) literature appear again until the 1500s or later.

The diary of **Lady Sarashina** (1009–1059), for instance, while clearly quite personal, is far outside the Western idea of self-analysis. Her expressions of her own feelings are muted, meaning that she does not state them plainly, but instead discusses a fleeting romance of her younger years in language that requires one to read between the lines. In fact this represents an attitude still common in Japan and other lands of East Asia, where people consider it rude to speak bluntly and directly. But, looking deeply into Lady Sarashina's recollections, one can find a tale of romance and unfulfilled longing.

King Shahriyar (SHAR-ee-yar) had to deal with difficulties in his love life, but the presentation of his story in ***The Thousand and One Nights*** could hardly be classified as a heartfelt tale of personal pain. That is not its purpose; rather, the story of King Shahriyar—how he came to distrust all women, and therefore decreed that he would sleep with a new wife each night, and have her beheaded the next morning—merely serves as a "frame" for some of the most exciting adventure tales of all time.

Audiences around the world have long enjoyed the yarns contained in *The Thousand and One Nights,* sometimes known as *The Arabian Nights*—among them "Ala-ed-Din [Aladdin] and the Wonderful Lamp," "Ali Baba and the Forty Thieves," and "Sinbad the Sailor." Almost as famous, however, is the "frame story" which provides a context for all the other tales. This is the saga of Shahrazad (SHAR-uh-zahd), or Sheherezade, the young bride who outwitted Shahriyar by telling him an enthralling tale each night, and saving the end for the following evening—at which time she would begin a new story as soon as she had finished the one before. Thus she saved her own life and that of other women, and won Shahriyar's love in the process.

Though *The Thousand and One Nights* offers a number of insights on male-female relations in the Muslim world, it is still pure fantasy. By contrast, the advice to women offered in the writings of **Christine de Pisan** (pee-ZAHN; 1364–c. 1430) and *The Goodman of Paris*—written by an anonymous Paris merchant in the 1390s—is quite practical and down-to-earth. Christine, the most well known female author of medieval times, wrote from the viewpoint of a woman, and offered women guidelines on how to manage their homes; the author of *The Goodman,* by contrast, wanted his wife to submit to his authority while performing her wifely duties. Along with the excerpts that precede them, these two writings present a varied look at personal life—and particularly the relations of men and women—during the Middle Ages.

Augustine

Excerpt from the Confessions
Published in *Confessions and Enchiridion*, 1955

Perhaps no figure in medieval Christianity was as admired and influential as Augustine (aw-GUS-tin; 354–430). Yet he was a man not only of the Middle Ages, but also of ancient times: he grew up in a world still dominated by the Western Roman Empire, but lived to see the beginning of its end. In this confused, changing environment, Augustine's writings presented an all-embracing view of Christian faith as the one solid rock in a sea of uncertainty.

Augustine grew up in North Africa, which was then part of the Roman Empire, and studied in Carthage. The latter city, located in what is now Tunisia, was a great center of learning—but it was also, as he made clear in his *Confessions,* a place where a young man could get into a great deal of mischief. While there, Augustine became involved in a number of sexual relationships, one of which resulted in the birth of a son; spent time with a gang of troublemakers called the "wreckers"; and flirted with a faith called Manichaeism (man-uh-KEE-izm), which the Church later declared a heresy (HAIR-uh-see), or a belief that goes against established teachings. But it was also in Carthage that Augustine was first set

"I was not in love as yet, but I was in love with love; and, from a hidden hunger, I hated myself for not feeling more intensely a sense of hunger. I was looking for something to love, for I was in love with loving."

Augustine

One of the most significant figures in the early history of the Church, Augustine or Aurelius Augustinus—who became recognized as St. Augustine after his death—helped bridge the period from ancient to medieval times. He grew up in a world heavily influenced by the Roman Empire, but the power of Rome had begun to fade in his time, and Augustine promoted Christian faith as a more stable foundation than any earthly kingdom.

Augustine was born in Tagaste (tuh-GAS-tee) in North Africa, and grew up studying traditional Roman subjects such as rhetoric (RET-ur-ik), or the art of speaking and writing. At home, his parents were divided on the subject of his religion: his father, Patricius, worshiped the old Roman gods, whereas his mother, Monica (later St. Monica) was a devout Christian. As Augustine later recalled in the *Confessions,* Monica prayed for him often during his wayward youth.

In his teens, he went away to school in Carthage, the greatest center of learning in the area. There he became involved with a woman, and fathered a son out of wedlock. He also flirted with Manichaeism (man-uh-KEE-izm), a religion against which he would argue passionately after he became a Christian. After his schooling in Carthage, Augustine became a teacher in that city and Tagaste, but he was frustrated with discipline problems in the schools, so he decided to move to Rome.

Augustine. *Reproduced by permission of the Library of Congress.*

Augustine arrived in Rome in 383, at the age of twenty-nine, and later moved to the north Italian town of Milan (mee-LAHN). There Monica joined him following the death of Patricius, who apparently converted to Christianity on his deathbed. Also in Milan, he came under the influence of Ambrose (St. Ambrose; 339–397), another important figure in the early Church. In July 386, Augustine converted to Christianity, and was baptized the following Easter.

Monica's happiness over her son's conversion was short-lived: as they were preparing to return to Tagaste in 391, she fell ill and died. So Augustine went back alone, to become first a priest and then, in 396, a bishop. In this capacity he acted as spiritual leader over the Christians at Hippo, a city in what is now Algeria, for the rest of his life.

on the path that led to his acceptance of Christianity more than ten years later.

Augustine went on to become one of the greatest defenders of the Christian faith, and after his death he was honored as a saint and early father of the Church. Yet in his *Confessions,* he laid bare his soul, showing the depths of his inner confusion and the many wrong things he had done in his youth. The book is addressed to God, and is one of the most deeply personal works ever written. In fact, it could be properly called the first real autobiography, or personal history, because it is not nearly as concerned with outside events as it is with the inner life of Augustine himself.

Things to remember while reading the excerpt from the *Confessions*

- As Augustine notes in the passage that follows, he became "a master in the School of Rhetoric" (RET-uh-rik)—that is, the art of writing and speaking. The first paragraph is among the most widely admired parts of the *Confessions,* and indeed of medieval literature, displaying as it does a finely tuned sense of balance: not only are his words well chosen, but his placement of them results in a finely crafted piece of literature. His love of rhetoric and learning, in fact, helped put him on the path to God: in the writings of Cicero (106–43 B.C.), a Roman orator or speaker, Augustine first discovered a hunger for higher things. The work to which he refers, the *Hortensius,* has been lost to history, and in fact most knowledge of it comes from Augustine's writings.

- Many young people can relate to Augustine's experience of having been "in love with love." In fact, much of what happened to him in Carthage sounds like a tale of troubled youth today: sexual experimentation, unwanted pregnancy, even a brief involvement with a street gang of sorts. The latter were the "wreckers," a group of young student hoodlums, but Augustine never became fully a part of the gang: compared to them, he says, he was "relatively sedate" or calm.

- The *Confessions* is addressed to God; hence Augustine's use of the second person (e.g., "you"), though in his case he uses the older *thou*. The passage is also filled with a clear sense of evil's existence: he refers, for instance, to his "obedience of devils, to whom I made offerings of my wicked deeds"—meaning that by committing sinful acts, he was serving the devil.

• At the time of the events described in this passage, Augustine was nineteen, and his father had died just two years before. This meant that his family's financial situation was shaky, and therefore he had to study "not to sharpen my tongue," but so that he could get a job. This passage is the only place in the *Confessions* where he even mentions the death of his father; by contrast, his mother was a major influence on him throughout his life. As Augustine makes clear throughout the book, in place of an earthly father he found God, the heavenly father.

Excerpt from the Confessions

Chapter I

*1. I came to Carthage, where a **caldron** of unholy loves was seething and bubbling all around me. I was not in love as yet, but I was in love with love; and, from a hidden hunger, I hated myself for not feeling more intensely a sense of hunger. I was looking for something to love, for I was in love with loving, and I hated security and a smooth way, free from snares. Within me I had a **dearth** of that inner food which is thyself, my God—although that dearth caused me no hunger. And I remained without any appetite for **incorruptible food**—not because I was already filled with it, but because the emptier I became the more I **loathed** it. Because of this my soul was unhealthy; and, full of sores, it **exuded itself forth**, itching to be scratched by scraping on the **things of the senses**. Yet, had these things no soul, they would certainly not inspire our love.*

To love and to be loved was sweet to me, and all the more when I gained the enjoyment of the body of the person I loved. Thus I pol-

Caldron (usually *cauldron*): A large pot.

Dearth: Lack.

Incorruptible food: Augustine is referring to spiritual, as opposed to physical, nourishment.

Loathed: Despised.

Exuded itself forth: Spread itself around.

Things of the senses: Things that provide physical or mental pleasure.

*luted the spring of friendship with the filth of **concupiscence** and I dimmed its **luster** with the slime of lust. Yet, foul and unclean as I was, I still craved, in excessive vanity, to be thought elegant and **urbane**. And I did fall **precipitately** into the love I was longing for. My God, my mercy, with how much bitterness didst thou, out of thy infinite goodness, flavor that sweetness for me! For I was not only beloved but also I secretly reached the climax of enjoyment; and yet **I was joyfully bound with troublesome tics**, so that I could be **scourged** with the burning iron rods of jealousy, suspicion, fear, anger, and strife....*

Chapter III

*5. And still thy faithful mercy hovered over me from afar. In what **unseemly iniquities** did I wear myself out, following a **sacrilegious** curiosity, which, having deserted thee, then began to drag me down into the treacherous **abyss**, into the **beguiling** obedience of devils, to whom I made offerings of my wicked deeds. And still in all this thou didst not fail to scourge me. I dared, even while thy solemn **rites** were being celebrated inside the walls of thy church, to desire and to plan a project which merited death as its fruit. For this thou didst chastise me with **grievous** punishments, but nothing in comparison with my fault, O thou my greatest mercy, my God, my refuge from those terrible dangers in which I wandered **with stiff neck**, **receding** farther from thee, loving my own ways and not thine—loving a **vagrant** liberty!*

*6. Those studies I was then pursuing, generally accounted as respectable, were aimed at distinction in the courts of law—to excel in which, the more crafty I was, the more I should be praised. Such is the blindness of men that they even glory in their blindness. And by this time I had become a master in the School of **Rhetoric**, and I rejoiced proudly in this honor and became inflated with arrogance. Still I was relatively **sedate**, O Lord, as thou knowest, and had no share in the wreckings of "The Wreckers" (for this stupid and **diabolical** name was regarded as the very badge of gallantry) among whom I lived with a sort of ashamed embarrassment that I was not even as they were. But I lived with them, and at times I was delighted with their friendship, even when I abhorred their acts (that is, their "wrecking") in which they insolently attacked the modesty of strangers, tormenting them by uncalled-for jeers, gratifying their mischievous mirth....*

Concupiscence: Sexual desire.

Luster (or *lustre*): Glow.

Urbane: Sophisticated or worldly.

Precipitately: Steeply.

I was joyfully bound with troublesome tics: In other words, "I enjoyed causing myself emotional pain."

Scourged: Whipped.

Unseemly: Improper.

Iniquities: Sins.

Sacrilegious: Displaying a strong lack of respect for God.

Abyss: A bottomless pit, like hell.

Beguiling: Misleading.

Rites: Religious ceremonies.

Grievous: Painful.

With stiff neck: Stubbornly.

Receding: Moving away.

Vagrant (adj.): Wandering or wayward.

Rhetoric: The art of writing and speaking.

Sedate: Calm.

Diabolical: Devilish.

Glossary

Eloquence: Ability to speak well.

Eminent: Great and honored.

Reprehensible: Not to be admired.

Vainglorious: Proud or haughty.

Exhortation: An appeal, or a call to action.

Philosophy: An area of study concerned with reaching a general understanding of human values and reality.

Not its style but its substance: Not the words or the way they were presented, but their meaning.

Ardent: Eager.

Chapter IV

*7. Among such as these, in that unstable period of my life, I studied the books of **eloquence**, for it was in eloquence that I was eager to be **eminent**, though from a **reprehensible** and **vainglorious** motive, and a delight in human vanity. In the ordinary course of study I came upon a certain book of Cicero's, whose language almost all admire, though not his heart. This particular book of his contains an **exhortation** to **philosophy** and was called Hortensius. Now it was this book which quite definitely changed my whole attitude and turned my prayers toward thee, O Lord, and gave me new hope and new desires. Suddenly every vain hope became worthless to me, and with an incredible warmth of heart I yearned for an immortality of wisdom and began now to arise that I might return to thee. It was not to sharpen my tongue further that I made use of that book. I was now nineteen; my father had been dead two years, and my mother was providing the money for my study of rhetoric. What won me in it [the Hortensius] was **not its style but its substance**.*

*8. How **ardent** was I then, my God, how ardent to fly from earthly things to thee! Nor did I know how thou wast even then dealing with me. For with thee is wisdom. In Greek the love of wisdom is called "philosophy," and it was with this love that that book inflamed me....*

What happened next ...

Augustine went on to become perhaps the greatest of the early Church fathers, men who established the foundations of medieval Christianity. During the last thirty-four years of his life, while serving as Bishop of Hippo, Augustine wrote hundreds of works, of which the *Confessions* and *City of God* (*De civitate*) are the most important.

The latter was a response to the sacking, or destruction, of Rome by an invading tribe called the Visigoths in 410. Whereas many Romans claimed that this misfortune had happened because they had rejected their old gods and embraced Christianity, Augustine argued that God was punishing them for exactly the opposite reason: because they had worshiped their idols for so long before embracing the true faith. Augustine died as his own adopted city of Hippo was being attacked by another tribe, the Vandals.

Did you know ...

- The city of Carthage that Augustine knew had been built on the site of another Carthage, destroyed by the Romans in 146 B.C. Founded by Phoenician (foh-NEE-shun) colonists in the 800s B.C., Carthage had been an extremely powerful city-state, and had vied with Rome itself for control of the western Mediterranean. The two cities fought a series of conflicts called the Punic (PYOO-nik) Wars, of which the most notable figure was Hannibal (247–183 B.C.), a general from Carthage who conducted a brilliant military campaign in Italy. When the Romans destroyed Carthage at the end of the Third Punic War, they sowed salt in the ground so that nothing would grow there; but 102 years later, in 44 B.C., Julius Caesar (100–44 B.C.) established the new city of Carthage.

- The oldest city in North America was named after Augustine: St. Augustine, Florida, founded by a Spanish explorer in 1565. The pronunciation of the names is different, however: Whereas Augustine's name is pronounced "aw-GUS-tin," St. Augustine is pronounced "AW-gus-teen."

- There is another extremely well known autobiography called the *Confessions,* this one by Jean-Jacques Rousseau (ZHAHN ZHAHK roo-SOH; 1712–1778). A French philosopher and author who had a tremendous impact on the French Revolution of 1789, Rousseau deliberately chose the title as a reference to Augustine's earlier work. He, too, talked about the reckless misadventures of his youth—but whereas Augustine was sorry for the things he had done, Rousseau seems to have taken pride in his youthful excesses.

A mosaic of Augustine (left); he lived to become a devout and influential Christian, but in his *Confessions* he describes his youthful doubt and confusion. *Reproduced by permission of the Corbis Corporation.*

For More Information

Books

Augustine. *Confessions and Enchiridion.* Translated and edited by Albert C. Outler. Philadelphia: Westminster Press, 1955.

De Zeeuw, P. *Augustine, the Farmer's Boy of Tagaste.* Pella, IA: Inheritance Publications, 1998.

Hansel, Robert R. *The Life of Saint Augustine.* New York: F. Watts, 1968.

Web Sites

Augustine: *Confessions.* [Online] Available http://ccel.org/a/augustine/confessions/confessions-bod.html (last accessed July 28, 2000).

Lady Sarashina

Excerpt from **The Diary of Lady Sarashina**
Published in *Diaries of Court Ladies of Old Japan,* **1920**

During the Heian period (hay-YAHN; 794–1185) of medieval Japan, when the capital was at Heian, or Kyoto, life in the Japanese imperial court began to turn inward. Nobles tended to look down on people outside the capital; hence Lady Sarashina (1009–1059) was embarrassed by the fact that she had lived in the country for part of her childhood, writing in her diary that "I am ashamed to think that inhabitants of the Royal City will think me an uncultured girl."

During this time, the division between city and country became so severe that the rural provinces functioned almost as separate countries. This period saw the rise of a feudal system much like that of medieval Europe, with landowners controlling peasant farmers through the military power of their knights or samurai. As with Europe in feudal times, there was a strongly romantic flavor to the world of samurai and noble ladies, an atmosphere reflected in many poems and other works of art.

Though men held most of the power, women enjoyed a lively cultural life of their own. The Heian period saw the writing of the world's first novel, the *Tale of Genji* by Lady

"That evening, after I had gone to my room, my companion came in to tell me that he had replied to my poem: 'If there be such a tranquil night as that of the rain, I should like in some way to make you listen to my lute, playing all the songs I can remember.'"

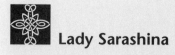

Lady Sarashina

Lady Sarashina was born in Kyoto, then the Japanese capital, but when she was nine years old her father became governor of a distant province. As a young girl, she became fascinated by romance novels, particularly the *Tale of Genji* by Lady Murasaki (c. 978–c. 1026). A novel is an extended work of fiction, and the *Tale of Genji* is generally regarded as the first of its kind. But Lady Sarashina seemed to later regret her interest in such stories: romantic tales, she suggested in her diary, did not prepare a woman for real life—and her own experiences appeared to bear this out.

When she was thirteen, her family returned to the capital, and later she became a lady-in-waiting, or attendant, to the princess Sadako. Sadako married a later emperor, and as the fortunes of the princess improved, so did those of Lady Sarashina. Yet when Sadako died in 1039, the emperor took a new wife, and Sarashina—who by then had become lady-in-waiting to Sadako's daughter—found herself outside the inner circle.

It was during this time, when she was in her early thirties, that she met, and had a brief romance with, the unnamed man described in the excerpt from her diaries. Later in her diary, she refers to a husband, but never indicates when she was married: apparently the husband came from a lower social rank than herself, and was such an embarrassment that she chose not to dwell on it. The end of her diary indicates that her latter years were not happy: "My people went to live elsewhere and I remained alone in my solitary home. I was tired of meditation and sent a poem to one who had not called on me for a long time [a friend who was a nun]: 'Weeds grow before my gate / And my sleeves are wet with dew, / No one calls on me, / My tears are solitary—alas!'"

Murasaki (c. 978–c. 1026). Lady Sarashina was heavily influenced by Lady Murasaki's story, as she confessed in her diary. It is not a diary in the Western sense, a day-by-day account of events: rather, it is a life story. Through their autobiographical writings, Japanese women—Lady Sarashina was one of several whose diaries have survived—found a rare opportunity to express their deepest feelings.

Things to remember while reading the excerpt from *The Diary of Lady Sarashina*

- The leadership of Heian Japan tried to separate themselves from everything that was not Japanese, but educated members of the court still took much of their cultural guidance from China's T'ang dynasty (TAHNG; 618–907). At the same time, however, the Japanese developed a number of artistic forms uniquely their own, among these a style of poetry noted for its subtlety, or delicate understatement. In order to fit in socially, a person of the upper classes had to display a keen knowledge of native poetic styles. Thus Lady Sarashina and the unnamed man spoke mainly of poetry, and addressed each other in poetic lines.

- Whereas many Americans are inclined to say exactly what they mean, this is not the case in most Asian societies—including that of medieval Japan. Therefore, to get the full meaning of Lady Sarashina's reflections on her brief love affair, one has to read between the lines. The man and Sarashina speak of love in a highly indirect fashion, and this was doubly so for Sarashina, as a woman: instead, she uses poetry to say things she cannot say directly.

- The events described in this passage took place over a two-year period that began when Lady Sarashina was thirty-three and serving as a lady-in-waiting, or attendant, at the royal court. Though thirty-three was a rather advanced age for a woman in those times to have been unmarried, as a lady of the court all of her attention was focused on the princess. Court ladies had little privacy, since they had to sleep near the royal person they attended; therefore it would have been difficult to maintain a marriage in such circumstances.

- The passage is peppered with references to Japanese culture, including traditions associated with the religions of Buddhism and Shinto, which in medieval times were

An illustration from Lady Murasaki's novel, the *Tale of Genji*. In her diary, Lady Sarashina admits to being heavily influenced by **Lady Murasaki.** *Reproduced by permission of the Corbis Corporation.*

practiced together. Thus there is mention of *sutras* (SOOT-ruz), or Buddhist sayings, and of the Shinto shrine at Ise (EE-say). Emperor Enyu, mentioned by Lady Sarashina's friend, reigned from 970 to 984.

Excerpt from The Diary of Lady Sarashina

... *On a very dark night in the beginning of the **Gods-absent month**, when sweet-voiced reciters were to read **sutras** throughout the night, another lady and I went out towards the entrance door of the **Audience Room** to listen to it, and after talking fell asleep, listening, leaning, ... when I noticed a gentleman had come to be received in audience by the Princess.*

"It is awkward to run away to our apartment [to escape him]. We will remain here. Let it be as it will." So said my companion and I sat beside her listening.

*He spoke gently and quietly. There was nothing about him to be regretted. "Who is the other lady?" he asked of my friend. He said nothing rude or **amorous** like other men, but talked delicately of the sad, sweet things of the world, and many a phrase of his with a strange power **enticed** me into conversation. He wondered that there should have been in the Court one who was a stranger to him, and did not seem inclined to go away soon.*

*There was no starlight, and a gentle shower fell in the darkness; how lovely was its sound on the leaves! "The more deeply beautiful is the night," he said; "the full moonlight would be too dazzling." **Discoursing** about the beauties of Spring and Autumn he continued: "Although every hour has its charm, pretty is the spring haze; then the sky being tranquil and overcast, the face of the moon is not too bright; it seems to be floating on a distant river. At such a time the calm spring melody of the **lute** is **exquisite**.*

*"In Autumn, on the other hand, the moon is very bright; though there are mists trailing over the horizon we can see things as clearly as if they were at hand. The sound of wind, the voices of insects, all sweet things seem to melt together. When at such a time we listen to the autumnal music of the **koto** we forget the Spring—we think that is best—*

Gods-absent month: October.

Sutras: Sayings based on the teachings of Buddhism.

Audience room: A place where a royal person receives visitors.

Amorous: Sexual.

Enticed: Attracted.

Discoursing: Talking.

Lute: A stringed instrument.

Exquisite: Nearly perfect.

Koto: A harp-like stringed instrument.

"But the winter sky frozen all over magnificently cold! The snow covering the earth and its light mingling with the moonshine! Then the notes of the **hitchiriki** vibrate on the air and we forget Spring and Autumn." And he asked us, "Which captivates your fancy? On which stays your mind?"

My companion answered in favour of Autumn and I, not being willing to imitate her, said:

> Pale green night and flowers all melting into one in the soft haze—
> Everywhere the moon, glimmering in the Spring night.

So I replied. And he, after repeating my poem to himself over and over, said: "Then you give up Autumn? After this, as long as I live, such a spring night shall be for me a memento of your personality." The person who favoured Autumn said, "Others seem to give their hearts to Spring, and I shall be alone gazing at the autumn moon."

He was deeply interested, and being uncertain in thought said: "Even the poets of the T'ang Empire could not decide which to praise most, Spring or Autumn. Your decisions make me think that there must be some personal reasons **when our inclination is touched or charmed.** Our souls are **imbued** with the colours of the sky, moon, or flowers of that moment. I desire much to know how you came to know the charms of Spring and Autumn. The moon of a winter night is given as an **instance** of dreariness, and as it is very cold I had never seen it intentionally. When I went down to Ise to be present as the messenger of the King at the ceremony of installing the virgin in charge of the **shrine**, I wanted to come back in the early dawn, so went to take leave of the Princess in a moon-bright night after many days' snow, half shrinking to think of my journey.

"Her residence was an other-worldly place **awful** even to the imagination, but she called me into an adequate apartment. There were persons [there] who had come down in the reign of the Emperor Enyu. Their aspect was very holy, ancient, and mystical. They told of the things of long ago with tears. They brought out a well-tuned four-stringed lute. The music **did not seem to be anything happening in this world**; I regretted that day should even dawn, and was touched so deeply that I had almost forgotten about returning to the Capital. Ever since then the snowy nights of winter recall that scene, and I without fail gaze at the

Hitchiriki: A reed pipe.

When our inclination is touched or charmed: In other words, when something appeals to us especially.

Imbued: Filled.

Instance: Example.

Shrine: A holy place for believers in a religion.

Awful: Awe-inspiring.

Did not seem to be anything happening in this world: In other words, it seemed like something from another world.

moon even though hugging the fire. You will surely understand me, and hereafter every dark night with gentle rain will touch my heart; I feel this has not been inferior to the snowy night at the palace of the Ise virgin."

With these words he departed and I thought he could not have known who I was.

In the Eighth month of the next year we went again to the Imperial Palace, and there was in the Court an entertainment throughout the night. I did not know that he was present at it, and I passed that night in my own room. When I looked out [in the early morning] opening the sliding doors on the corridor I saw the morning moon very faint and beautiful. I heard footsteps and people approached—some reciting sutras. One of them came to the entrance, and addressed me. I replied, and he, suddenly remembering, exclaimed, "That night of softly falling rain I do not forget, even for a moment! I yearn for it." As chance did not permit me many words I said:

> *What intensity of memory clings to your heart?*
> *That gentle shower fell on the leaves*
> **Only for a moment.**

I had scarcely said so when people came up and I stole back without his answer.

That evening, after I had gone to my room, my companion came in to tell me that he had replied to my poem: "If there be such a tranquil night as that of the rain, I should like in some way to make you listen to my lute, playing all the songs I can remember."

I wanted to hear it, and waited for the fit occasion, but there was none, ever.

In the next year one tranquil evening I heard that he had come into the Princess's Palace, so I crept out of my chamber with my companion, but there were many people waiting within and without the Palace, and I turned back. He must have been of the same mind with me. He had come because it was so still a night, and he returned because it was noisy.

> *I yearn for a tranquil moment*
> *To be out upon the sea of harmony,*
> *In that enchanted boat.*
> *Oh, boatman, do you know my heart?*

Only for a moment: The unspoken idea here is that for a moment, their hearts were as one.

*So I composed that poem—and there is nothing more to tell. His personality was very excellent and he was not an ordinary man, but time passed, and **neither called to the other**....*

Neither called to the other: In other words, "we never met again."

What happened next ...

As Lady Sarashina indicated, the romance went no further. Apparently she later married and had children with a man for whom she did not feel nearly as great an attraction as she had for the stranger at the palace. She spent her final years away from the capital, and apparently died unhappy.

The Heian period lasted long after her death in 1059, and though it was a time of great cultural advancement in Japan, it was also a troubled era characterized by near-constant warfare. Even greater confusion followed, as a series of *shoguns* or military dictators took power after 1185. Japan did not become fully unified until 1573.

Did you know ...

- Later Europeans would claim credit for developing the novel as a literary form, and would attribute its creation to male authors of the Renaissance, but in fact the world's first novel was the *Tale of Genji,* written by Lady Murasaki between 1001 and 1015. It tells the story of a character named Prince Genji with astounding subtlety and complexity of plot, and the romantic elements of the story had a great influence on young women such as Lady Sarashina. The *Tale of Genji* is still widely read today.

- Samurai, which appeared in Japan during the Heian period, were the equivalent of European knights: instead of fighting in mass military formations, they were heavily armed individual warriors. Their armor was made of bamboo and not metal, however, and they placed a greater emphasis on the sword than knights did. In Europe, lances and crossbows made it possible to fight at a greater distance, but combat in Japan was face-to-face, and swords were so sharp they could slice a man's body in half with a single stroke.

For More Information

Books

Murasaki Shikibu (Lady Murasaki). *The Tale of Genji* (abridged). New York: Knopf, 1993.

Omori, Annie Shepley and Kochi Doi, translators. *Diaries of Court Ladies of Old Japan*. Boston: Houghton Mifflin, 1920.

Lady Sarashina. *As I Crossed a Bridge of Dreams: Reflections of a Woman in Eleventh-Century Japan*. Translated by Ivan Morris. New York: Penguin USA, 1989.

Web Sites

"Sarashina." *Hanover Historical Texts Project*. [Online] Available http://history.hanover.edu/texts/diaries/diaryall.htm (last accessed July 28, 2000).

The Thousand and One Nights

Excerpt from **The Thousand and One Nights**
Published in *Stories from the Thousand and One Nights:*
The Arabian Night's Entertainments, **1937**

The Thousand and One Nights, better known in the West as *The Arabian Nights,* almost needs no introduction. There is hardly a person alive who has not been enthralled by one of its tales, particularly the three most famous: "Ala-ed-Din [Aladdin] and the Wonderful Lamp," "Ali Baba and the Forty Thieves," and "Sinbad the Sailor." Out of the hundreds of other tales that form the book, perhaps the most well known is the "frame story"—that is, the story that provided a larger context or meaning for all the tales.

It seems that a certain king came to distrust all women after he discovered that his wife had been unfaithful to him. He therefore resolved to sleep with a different wife every night, then have her beheaded in the morning. But one wife, Shahrazad (SHAR-uh-zahd) or Sheherazade (shuh-HAIR-uh-zahd), outsmarted him. On her first night with him, she began telling a tale, but when dawn came she was not finished. The king was intrigued, and therefore he kept her alive until the next night—when she would do the same thing again. She kept this up over the course of more than three years, during which time she produced three male heirs, and at the end of

> "The King, hearing these words, and being restless, was pleased with the idea of listening to the story; and thus, on the first night of the thousand and one, Shahrazad commenced her recitations."

73

The Thousand and One Nights

Better known in the West as *The Arabian Nights,* the collection of tales known as *The Thousand and One Nights* delighted audiences in the Middle East for centuries before Europeans discovered them. The tales had no single author or source; rather, they were collected from Persian, Indian, and Arabian stories that had been passed down orally for generations.

The first collected version of 264 tales appeared in Persia (modern Iran) during the A.D. 900s. By that time, the "frame story" concerning Shahrazad (SHAR-uh-zahd)—a version of which is excerpted here—had been added to provide a larger context or meaning for all the tales. Over time, new stories were added, and by about 1450 the tales had assumed more or less their present form.

1,001 nights, the king gave up on his original plan and let her live.

From the standpoint of personal and individual life, the frame story is interesting for what it reveals about men and women. In almost any culture, it is a man's ultimate humiliation to discover that his wife has been cheating on him, but the Muslim world of the Middle East was (and is) even more male-dominated than most societies; thus the king's humiliation at discovering his first wife's unfaithfulness was all the worse. And given the striking imbalance of male and female power that prevailed in that place and time, Shahrazad's calm wisdom is all the more impressive.

Things to remember while reading the excerpt from *The Thousand and One Nights*

- Though the sources of *The Thousand and One Nights* include tales from Persia (modern-day Iran), India, and Arabia, the tale of Shahrazad is almost certainly Persian. One way scholars know this is through the names, which are drawn from Farsi, the Persian language. Shahriyar (SHAR-ee-yar), the name of the king, means "friend of the city"; and his brother's name, Shah-Zeman, means "king of the age." Samarkand (sah-mur-KAHND) is an ancient city on the Old Silk Road, a trade route that connected Europe, the Middle East, and the Far East. Today it is part of Uzbekistan, a nation in Central Asia.

- The following passage has been significantly condensed; the original is four times as long, containing lengthy descriptions of Shahriyar's wealth, the Wezir's (or government official's) trip to see Shah-Zeman, and other details not important to the larger story. After Shahriyar returns from his hunting trip and discovers that his wife has been cheating, he and Shah-Zeman travel far away and meet a woman who also cheats on her "man"—only this man is a genie. After this, they return, and Shahriyar kills his wife. Also, before Shahrazad's father allows her to marry Shahriyar, he tells a lengthy story that has also been omitted.

- Despite the collection's reputation as tales for children, *The Thousand and One Nights* contains a number of stories that should be labeled "Parental Discretion Advised." The following passage hints at a number of sexual details that are presented more openly in other tales from the collection.

- Modern readers may find racist overtones in the fact that when the wives of both Shah-Zeman and Shahriyar cheat on their husbands, it is with black slaves. There was an unquestionable tension between the Muslim peoples of the Middle East and African slaves, who they called "Zanj," and this probably influenced the depiction in this story. However, if a person chose only to read things that agreed with the prevailing morality of their own time, many valuable books from the past would be off-limits. Also, it is always worthwhile to be reminded that Europeans and their descendants in America are not the only people who have been guilty of racism.

An illustration from "Sinbad the Sailor," one of many famous tales from *The Thousand and One Nights*, also known as *The Arabian Nights*. *Reproduced by permission of the Corbis Corporation.*

Excerpt from The Thousand and One Nights

... It is related (but God alone is all-knowing, as well as all-wise, and almighty, and all-bountiful), that there was, in ancient times, a

*King of the countries of India and China, possessing numerous troops, and guards, and servants, and domestic dependents.... He was called King Shahriyar: his younger brother was named Shah-Zeman, and was King of Samarkand. The administration of their governments was conducted with **rectitude**, each of them ruling over his subjects with justice during a period of twenty years with the utmost enjoyment and happiness. After this period, the elder King felt a strong desire to see his brother, and ordered his **Wezir** to **repair** to him and bring him....*

*[Having been thus summoned by his brother, Shah-Zeman] ... sent forth his tents and camels and mules and servants and guards, appointed his Wezir to be governor of the country during his absence, and set out towards his brother's **dominions**. At midnight, however, he remembered that he had left in his palace an article which he should have brought with him; and having returned to the palace to fetch it, he there beheld his wife sleeping in his bed, and attended by a male negro slave, who had fallen asleep by her side.*

*On beholding this scene, the world became black before his eyes; and he said within himself, If this is the case when I have not departed from the city, what will be the conduct of this vile woman while I am **sojourning** with my brother? He then drew this sword, and slew them both in the bed: after which he immediately returned, gave orders for departure, and journeyed to his brother's capital.*

*Shahriyar, rejoicing at the tidings of his approach, went forth to meet him, **saluted him**, and welcomed him with the utmost delight. He then ordered that the city should be decorated on the occasion, and sat down to entertain his brother with cheerful conversation: but the mind of King Shah-Zeman was distracted by reflections upon the conduct of his wife.... His brother observed his altered condition, and, imagining that it was occasioned by his absence from his dominions, **abstained** from troubling him or asking respecting the cause, until after the lapse of some days.... Shahriyar then said, I wish that thou wouldest go out with me on a hunting excursion; perhaps thy mind might so be diverted. But he declined; and Shahriyar went alone to the **chase**.*

Now there were some windows in the King's palace commanding a view of his garden; and while his brother was looking out from one of these, a door of the palace was opened, and there came forth from it twenty females and twenty male black slaves; and the King's wife, who was distinguished by extraordinary beauty and elegance, accompanied them to a fountain, where they all disrobed them-

Rectitude: Rightness or justice.

Wezir (or vizier): A high governmental official.

Repair: Go.

Dominions: Lands.

Sojourning: Staying.

Saluted him: Waved to him.

Abstain: To force oneself not to do something.

Chase: Hunt.

selves, and sat down together. The King's wife then called out, O Mes'ud! and immediately a black slave came to her, and embraced her; she doing the like....

When his brother returned from his excursion, and they had saluted each other.... [Shah-Zeman] repeated to him all that he had seen. I would see this, said Shahriyar, with my own eye. Then, said Shah-Zeman, **give out** *that thou art going again to the chase, and conceal thyself here with me, and thou shalt witness this conduct, and* **obtain ocular proof** *of it.*

Shahriyar, upon this, immediately announced that it was his intention to make another excursion. The troops went out of the city with the tents, and the King followed them; and after he had reposed awhile in the camp, he said to his servants, Let no one come in to me. And he disguised himself, and returned to his brother in the palace, and sat in one of the windows overlooking the garden; and when he had been there a short time, the women and their mistress entered the garden with the black slaves, and did as his brother had described, continuing so until the hour of the afternoon-prayer.

... Shahriyar caused his wife to be beheaded, and in like manner the women and black slaves; and thenceforth he made it his regular custom, every time that he took a virgin to his bed, to kill her at the expiration of the night. Thus he continued to do during a period of three years; and the people raised an outcry against him, and fled with their daughters, and there remained not a virgin in the city of a sufficient age for marriage. Such was the case when the King ordered the Wezir to bring him a virgin according to his custom; and the Wezir went forth and searched, and found none; and he went back to his house enraged and **vexed**, *fearing what the King might do to him.*

Now the Wezir had two daughters; the elder of whom was named Shahrazad; and the younger, Dunyzad. The former had read various books of histories, and the lives of preceding kings, and stories of past generations: it is asserted that she had collected together a thousand books of histories, relating to preceding generations and kings, and works of the poets: and she said to her father on this occasion, Why do I see thee thus changed, and oppressed with solicitude and sorrows? It has been said by one of the poets:

Tell him who is oppressed with anxiety, that anxiety will not last: As happiness passeth away, so passeth away anxiety.

When the Wezir heard these words from his daughter, he related to her all that had happened to him with regard to the King:

Give out: Spread the word.

Obtain ocular proof: In other words, "see it with your own eyes."

Vexed: Worried.

upon which she said, By Allah, O my father, give me in marriage to this King: either I shall die, and be a ransom for one of the daughters of the Muslims, or I shall live, and be the cause of their deliverance from him. **I conjure thee by Allah,** *exclaimed he, that thou expose not thyself to such peril. But she said, It must be so....*

... Now she had given directions to her younger sister saying to her, When I have gone to the King, I will send to request thee to come; and when thou comest to me, and seest a convenient time, do thou say to me, O my sister, relate to me some strange story to **beguile our waking hour.** *And I will relate to thee a story that shall, if it be the will of God, be the means of procuring deliverance.*

Her father, the Wezir, then took her to the King, who, when he saw him, was rejoiced, and said, Hast thou brought me what I desired? He answered Yes. When the King, therefore, introduced himself to her, she wept; and he said to her, What aileth thee? She answered, O King, I have a young sister, and I wish to take leave of her. So the King sent to her; and she [Dunyzad] came to her sister, and em-

I conjure thee by Allah: In other words, "I command you in God's name."

Beguile our waking hour: In other words, "to pass the time."

braced her, and sat near the foot of the bed; and after she had waited for a proper opportunity, she said, By Allah! O my sister, relate to us a story to beguile the waking hour of our night. Most willingly, answered Shahrazad, if this virtuous King permit me. And the King, hearing these words, and being restless, was pleased with the idea of listening to the story; and thus, on the first night of the thousand and one, Shahrazad commenced her recitations.

What happened next ...

Shahrazad, as the story eventually reveals, outwitted Shahriyar, stringing him along for more than three years. By then she had given him three sons, and the king, who had come to love her deeply, abandoned his earlier plan to kill off his wives.

The first translation of *The Thousand and One Nights* into a European language appeared in the early 1700s, thanks to the French scholar Antoine Galland (an-TWAHN guh-LAWn; 1646–1715). Galland added several stories he had collected from other Middle Eastern sources—stories not found in

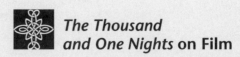

The Thousand and One Nights on Film

More than a hundred movies about *The Thousand and One Nights*, or one of its tales, have been filmed over the years—including a version of *Ali Baba* released in 1907. One of the most well known ones among modern audiences, of course, is Disney's *Aladdin* (1992), but that is only one of some fifty movies concerning "Aladdin and the Wonderful Lamp." Half as many more films concern "Sinbad the Sailor," and an equal number focus on "Ali Baba and the Forty Thieves."

A sampling of titles illustrates the wide appeal of *The Thousand and One Nights: Ali-Baba und die 40 Räuber* (Germany, 1922); *Popeye the Sailor Meets Ali Baba's Forty Thieves* (United States, 1937); *Sinbad contro i sette saraceni* (*Sinbad Against the Seven Saracens,* Italy, 1964); *Senya ichiya monogatari* (*One Thousand and One Arabian Nights,* Japan, 1969); *Priklyucheniya Ali-Baby i soroka razboynikov* (*Adventures of Ali Baba and the Forty Thieves,* Soviet Union, 1979); and *Scooby Doo in Arabian Nights* (United States, 1994).

the original versions of *The Thousand and One Nights*. Among these are two of the most famous: "Ali Baba and the Forty Thieves" and "Ala-ed-Din [Aladdin] and the Wonderful Lamp."

The Thousand and One Nights has added immeasurably to the shared culture of the world, providing people in the Middle East, Europe, and other places with a common set of stories and symbols. Because of these stories' popularity, half the world knows about genies, magic carpets and lamps, and the phrase "open sesame." The stories have also greatly expanded awareness of Middle Eastern culture, and of the Islamic religion, among peoples of other cultures.

Did you know ...

- One of the most beloved pieces of music in the world is *Sheherazade* (1888), a suite, or series of pieces, by the Russian composer Nikolai Rimsky-Korsakov (NEE-koh-ly RIM-skee KOHR-suh-kawf; 1844–1908). Various sections of the suite provide musical representations of different stories, such as that of Sinbad. Throughout, a gentle violin indicates the voice of Shahrazad, telling her tales.

- Use of frame stories goes back all the way to the *Metamorphosis* by the Roman poet Ovid (AH-vid; 43 B.C.–A.D. 17). In medieval times, it made notable appearances not only in *The Thousand and One Nights,* but in the *Decameron* of Boccaccio (boh-KAHT-choh; 1313–1375) and the *Canterbury Tales* of Geoffrey Chaucer (c. 1342–1400). In modern times, frames have been used in works such as "The Celebrated Jumping Frog of Calaveras County" by Mark Twain (1835–1910) or the movies *The Princess Bride* (1987) and *Fried Green Tomatoes* (1991). In these modern works, the frame wraps only one story, not many; and in the last example, the characters in the frame story continue to develop along with those in the "main" tale.

For More Information

Books

Burton, Richard Francis. *The Arabian Nights' Entertainments, or the Book of A Thousand Nights and a Night: A Selection of the Most Representative of These Tales.* Edited by Bennett Cerf. New York: Modern Library, 1997.

Lane, Edward William, translator. *Stories from the Thousand and One Nights: The Arabian Night's Entertainments.* Revised by Stanley Lane-Poole. New York: Collier, 1937.

One Thousand and One Arabian Nights. Translated by Geraldine McCaughrean. New York: Oxford University Press, 1996.

Stewart, Desmond and The Editors of Time-Life Books. *Early Islam.* New York: Time-Life Books, 1967.

Web Sites

"Thousand and One Nights." *BiblioBytes.* [Online] Available http://www. bb.com/looptestlive.cfm?bookid=796&startow=2 (last accessed July 28, 2000).

Christine de Pisan

Excerpt from The Treasure of the City of Ladies
Published in 1985

The Goodman of Paris

Excerpt from The Goodman of Paris
Published in 1928

In the 1300s and 1400s, as Europe passed from the Middle Ages into the beginnings of the Renaissance (RIN-uh-sah-nts), trade was increasing, cities were growing, and a new middle and working class appeared. Both groups, an essential part of a growing economy, fell between the rich and the poor: the middle class were typically owners of small businesses, and the working class were less educated (and usually less wealthy) people who worked with their hands.

As contact between various classes increased, so did awareness of social rank and the need for rules governing such contact. This was particularly important with regard to relationships between men and women. Here class barriers were not so important as were traditional male and female roles, though it appears that the author of *The Goodman of Paris* had married a woman of a higher class. This, along with the fact that she was a teenager and he was clearly a man much older, indicates that he may have felt a need to keep her under control, as the excerpt from his instructions to her suggests. (The term "goodman" was a medieval word meaning "master of the house"; as for the author of *The*

"And besides encouraging the others, the wife herself should be involved in the work to the extent that she knows all about it, so that she may know how to oversee his workers if her husband is absent, and to reprove them if they do not do well."

From The Treasure of the City of Ladies

"I have often wondered how I might find a simple general introduction to teach you.... [M]e-seems that ... it can be accomplished in this way, namely in a general instruction that I will write for you."

From The Goodman of Paris

Christine de Pisan (kneeling) offers a manuscript to Isabel of Bavaria, Queen of France.
Reproduced by permission of the Corbis Corporation.

Goodman of Paris, he was an anonymous Paris merchant of the 1390s.)

Christine de Pisan (pee-ZAHN; sometimes spelled Pizan; 1364–c. 1430), perhaps the most well known female author of medieval times, offered a different view of marital relations in a passage called "Of the Wives of Artisans and How They Ought to Conduct Themselves," from *The Treasure of the City of Ladies.*

Christine de Pisan

The trials of single motherhood, making a living in a male-dominated world, trying to raise a family on the income of a working mom—these all sound like problems specific to many modern women, but in fact they characterized the career of Christine de Pisan.

Born in the Italian city of Venice, Christine was raised in the court of France's King Charles V (ruled 1364–80), for whom her father worked as court astrologer. When she was fifteen, she married the king's secretary, Étienne du Castel (ay-tee-AN). By the time Christine was twenty-five years old, however, she had lost not only her husband, but her father and her king. Not only that, but she had three children to raise.

Christine continued to serve in the French court, which was her "day job," but she also began to write poems and other works for patrons, or wealthy supporters. She went on to become perhaps the best-known female writer of the Middle Ages, and in her work she defended the status of women against many outspoken male critics. Among her notable writings were *The Book of the Three Virtues,* also known as *The Treasure of the City of Ladies;* an autobiography called *The Vision of Christine;* and a poem celebrating another notable woman of fifteenth-century France, Joan of Arc.

She depicted a situation in which neither age nor class separated a husband and wife, and she took for granted the fact that the power in the home resided in the hands of the woman. Perhaps this was the secret view of the Goodman, which would further explain his need to control his young wife.

Things to remember while reading the excerpts from *The Treasure of the City of Ladies* and *The Goodman of Paris*

- Both passages illustrate a high awareness of social class or rank. The author of *The Goodman of Paris,* for instance, takes note of the fact that his young wife came from a higher class than he; no doubt her family had fallen on hard times, and she was forced to marry him for financial support. Similarly, Christine de Pisan specifically addresses the wives of artisans, skilled workers who might be part of either the middle or the working class.

- These two writings appeared within a few years of one another, around the end of the 1300s and the beginning of the 1400s. Both suggest the changing economic climate of the times, as Western Europe began to prosper and new classes—primarily the middle class and the working class—began to divide the very rich from the very poor. The Goodman of Paris appears to have been a moderately wealthy merchant, and though the artisans' wives addressed by Christine de Pisan were certainly not rich, the fact that their husbands employed other workers implies that they were not poor either.

- The Goodman's reference to his young bride as "sister" is simply a term of affection. As for her marriage at age fifteen to a man who was clearly many years older than she, this was nothing unusual during the Middle Ages.

Fifteenth-century manuscript illustration from Christine de Pisan's *The City of Ladies*, a work that was followed by *The Treasure of the City of Ladies*. Reproduced by permission of the Corbis Corporation.

Excerpt from
The Treasure of the City of Ladies

*Now it is time for us to speak of the station in life of women married to **artisans** who live in cities and fine towns, like Paris, and elsewhere.... All wives of artisans should be very **painstaking** and diligent if they wish to have the necessities of life. They should encourage their husbands or their workmen to get to work early in the morning and work until late, for mark our words, there is no trade so good that if you neglect your work you will not have difficulty putting bread on the table. And besides encouraging the others, the wife herself should be involved in the work to the extent that she knows all about it, so that she may know how to oversee his work-*

Artisans: Skilled workers who produce items according to their specialty.

Painstaking: Careful.

ers if her husband is absent, and to **reprove** them if they do not do well. She ought to oversee them to keep them from idleness, for through careless workers the master is sometimes ruined. And when customers come to her husband and try to drive a hard bargain, she ought to warn him **solicitously** to take care that he does not make a bad deal. She should advise him to be **chary** of **giving too much credit** if he does not know precisely where and to whom it is going, for in this way many come to poverty, although sometimes the greed to earn more or to accept a tempting proposition makes them do it.

In addition, she ought to keep her husband's love as much as she can, **to this end:** that he will stay at home more willingly and that he may not have any reason to join the foolish crowds of other young men in **taverns** and indulge in unnecessary and extravagant expense, as many tradesmen do, especially in Paris. By treating him kindly she should protect him as well as she can from this. It is said that three things drive a man from his home: a quarrelsome wife, a smoking fireplace and a leaking roof. She too ought to stay at home gladly and not go every day **traipsing hither and yon** gossiping with the neighbours and visiting her chums to find out what everyone is doing. This is done by **slovenly** housewives roaming about the town in groups. Nor should she go off on these **pilgrimages** got up for no good reason and involving a lot of needless expense. Furthermore, she ought to remind her husband that they should live so **frugally** that their expenditure does not exceed their income, so that at the end of the year they do not find themselves in debt.

Excerpt from The Goodman of Paris

DEAR SISTER,

*You being the age of fifteen years and in the week that you and I were wed, did pray me to be **indulgent** to your youth and to your **small and ignorant service**, until you had seen and learned more; to this end you promised me to give all heed and to set all care and diligence to keep my peace and my love, as you spoke full wisely, and as I well believe, **with other wisdom than your own, beseeching** me humbly in our bed, as I remember, for the love of God not to correct you harshly before strangers nor before our own folk, but rather each night, or from day to day, in our chamber, to remind you of the **unseemly** or foolish things done in the day or days past, and **chastise** you, if it pleased me, and then you would **strive** to **amend** yourself according to my teaching and correction, and to serve my will in all things, as you said.... [Y]our youth excuses your **unwisdom** and*

Reprove: Rebuke or correct.

Solicitously: With great concern.

Chary: Cautious.

Giving too much credit: In other words, allowing too many customers to buy items on credit (i.e., with promises to pay later).

To this end: With this purpose in mind.

Taverns: Bars.

Traipsing: Walking.

Hither and yon: Here and there.

Slovenly: Careless, untidy.

Pilgrimage: A journey to a sacred place or shrine; this was a popular practice in the Middle Ages.

Frugally: Inexpensively.

Indulgent: Forgiving, patient.

Small and ignorant service: Limited experience.

With other wisdom than your own: In other words, on the basis of wisdom she had been taught, not simply things she already knew.

Beseeching: Begging.

Unseemly: Inappropriate or improper.

Chastise: Rebuke or correct.

Strive: Make an effort.

Amend: Change.

Unwisdom: Lack of wisdom.

*will still excuse you in all things as long as all you do is with good intent and not displeasing to me. And know that I am pleased rather than displeased that you tend rose-trees, and care for violets ... and dance, and sing: nor would I have you cease to do so among our friends and equals, and it is but good and seemly so to pass the time of your youth, so long as you neither seek nor try to go to the feasts and dances of lords of too high rank, for that does not become you, nor does it sort with **your estate** nor mine.... For although I know well that you are of gentler birth than I, **natheless** that would not protect you, for by God, the women of your **lineage** be good enough to correct you harshly themselves, if I did not, and they learnt of your error from me or from another source; but in you I have no fear, I have confidence in your good intent.... And for your honour and love, and **not for my service** (for to me belongs but the common service, or less), since I had pity and loving compassion on you who for long have had neither father nor mother, nor any of your **kinswoman** near you to whom you might turn for counsel in your private needs, save me alone, for whom you were brought from your **kin** and the country of your birth, I have often wondered how I might find a simple general introduction to teach you.... And lastly, **me-seems** that if your love is as it has appeared in your good words, it can be accomplished in this way, namely in a general instruction that I will write for you ... in three sections containing nineteen principal articles....*

What happened next ...

As the 1400s progressed, the economic and social changes mirrored in the writings of Christine de Pisan and the anonymous *Goodman of Paris* began to accelerate. Prior to the expansion of Europe's economy, which started after the Crusades began opening international trade in about 1100, there had been only two classes in European society: the very rich and the very poor. Now there was a growing array of classes, which presented new challenges for society as a whole.

Among these challenges was the fact that the status of women in the higher classes tended to improve much faster than that of women in the lower classes. For instance, a beggar in London or Paris might be considered the lowest of the low, yet if he had a wife, there was always someone even lower than he. By contrast, the wife of a wealthy merchant might be expected to submit to her husband, but she in turn had full power to command servants and other workers—male as well as female.

It is not surprising, then, that Christine de Pisan herself came from a high social class. One would be hard-pressed to come up with the name of a poor woman from the Middle Ages, except perhaps the peasant girl Joan of Arc—who was an exceptional person by any standard. Poor women were typically too busy just making a living, and that, combined with the fact that few poor people of either sex could read and write, meant that few ever gained distinction. Only in the late 1800s, as a rising tide of social consciousness turned more attention toward neglected groups, did society begin to lend an ear to its poor, and to women of all classes.

Courtesy Books

Courtesy books, which appeared in medieval Europe from the 1100s onward, may well have been the world's first self-help literature. These were manuals that taught people how to behave politely—a rare skill at a time when most Europeans were unclean and uncouth.

Some courtesy books taught pages, young boys in training for knighthood, how to behave like little men rather than boys; and others provided squires, teenagers who hoped to become knights, with instruction on manly virtues such as bravery. Knights also had their courtesy books, such as *Book of the Order of Chivalry* by Ramon Llull (LYOOL; c. 1235–1316) of Spain. In addition, there were courtesy books for women, and for various groups in society such as merchants or skilled workers.

Did you know ...

- The first sentence from *The Goodman of Paris* excerpt is a run-on, and consists of 166 words.

- A man once complained to Christine de Pisan that because there were so few educated women, educated women were unappealing—implying that because he had far fewer chances of meeting one who was educated, he might as well concentrate on the ones who were not. Christine retorted that she found ignorant men even less appealing—precisely because there were so many of them.

- *The Goodman of Paris* offers a wealth of insight concerning the medieval mind, providing information, for instance, on how to protect oneself against witchcraft. Its author also presented his wife with a dozen ways to get rid of flies.

• A saying quoted by Christine de Pisan was apparently quite popular at the time: in a later passage from *The Goodman of Paris,* its author counsels his wife to "remember the rustic [old] proverb, which saith that there be three things which drive the goodman from home, to wit a leaking roof, a smoky chimney and a scolding woman."

For More Information

Books

Ashby, Ruth and Deborah Gore Ohrn, editors. *Herstory: Women Who Changed the World.* Introduction by Gloria Steinem. New York: Viking, 1995.

Christine de Pisan. *The Treasure of the City of Ladies.* Translated by Sarah Lawson. New York: Penguin, 1985.

The Goodman of Paris. Translated by Eileen Power. London: Routledge, 1928.

McLeod, Enid. *The Order of the Rose: The Life and Ideas of Christine de Pizan.* London: Chatto & Windus, 1976.

Willard, Charity Cannon. *Christine de Pizan: Her Life and Works.* New York: Persea Books, 1984.

Web Sites

"Christine de Pizan." [Online] Available http://www.millersv.edu/~english/homepage/duncan/medfem/pizanhp.html (last accessed July 28, 2000).

"Medieval Sourcebook: *The Goodman of Paris* 1392/4." *Medieval Sourcebook.* [Online] Available http://www.fordham.edu/halsall/source/goodman.html (last accessed July 28, 2000).

Church and State

3

"Church and state" is another term for "religion and government." Both are powerful and influential forces that sometimes find themselves in conflict, a conflict that still concerns people today. For instance, many Christians in America believe that public schools should hold prayer each morning, whereas a wide array of people in groups such as the American Civil Liberties Union (ACLU) oppose this on the grounds that it goes against "the separation of church and state." This expression refers to the fact that in America, no religious body is allowed to dominate the government. Though they do not agree on what "separation of church and state" means, most Americans agree with the basic principle. This was not the case in the Middle Ages, a time when people had no concept of separation between religion and government.

The relationship between the Catholic Church and the governments of medieval Western Europe became so strong, in fact, that it was hard to imagine a time when the two were not linked. Certainly there had been a connection between government and religion of some kind since history began, but only with the emperor Constantine (KAHN-stun-teen; ruled 306–37) in 312 did Rome abandon its old gods in favor of Christianity.

After the Western Roman Empire fell in 476, the popes—spiritual and political leaders of the Catholic Church—needed to make an alliance with one of the kings from among the "barbarian" or uncivilized tribes that had taken Rome's place. But most of these barbarian kings had embraced a form of Christianity called Arianism, which the Catholic Church had declared a heresy (HAIR-uh-see), or something that goes against established Church teaching.

Thus the conversion of Clovis (ruled 481–511), king of a tribe called the Franks, to mainstream Christianity was a particularly significant event. As **Gregory of Tours** (TOOR; 538–594) wrote in his *History of the Franks,* Clovis had married a Christian wife, but had long rejected her religion until the day when he found himself losing a battle with a rival tribe. Clovis called on the Christian God's help, Gregory wrote, and won the battle, whereupon he and his people converted to Christianity. The Franks, who gave their name to the nation of France, went on to become the dominant power in Europe.

In 800, a pope crowned the Frankish king Charlemagne (SHAHR-luh-main; ruled 768–814) as "Emperor of the Romans," thus in effect creating a new Roman Empire linked to the Catholic Church. The Holy Roman Empire, as it came to be known, was never more than a collection of smaller states within what is now Germany and surrounding countries, but it was a powerful idea, and eventually the Holy Roman emperors came to see themselves as figures on a par with the popes.

The two forces vied for leadership of Western Europe, and this struggle came to a head in a conflict between **Emperor Henry IV** (ruled 1056–1106) and **Pope Gregory VII** (ruled 1073–1085). When Gregory ordered Henry to stop appointing bishops, church leaders with authority over the priests and believers in a given region, Henry responded with an angry letter in which he denounced Gregory as a "false monk." Gregory in turn issued orders to Henry's subjects that they were no longer required to obey him.

In the struggle between Henry and Gregory, neither man came out the winner, though in the end it appeared that the Church had triumphed over the state. In 1095, Pope Urban II (ruled 1088–99) launched the first of many crusades, wars intended to win back control of the Holy Land or Palestine from the Muslims who controlled it. Two centuries later, however, in the time of **Dante Alighieri** (DAHN-tay al-eeg-YEER-ee; 1265–1321), the enthusiasm that fueled the Crusades had been spent. Much of Dante's *Divine Comedy,* a classic of world literature, was concerned with corruption among the religious leadership of his time, which saw a shift in power away from the Church and toward the political leaders of Europe.

So far the relationship between Church and state has been discussed purely in terms of the West, or cultures influenced by ancient Greece and Rome. But the relationship of religion and politics was no less powerful in the East, as illustrated by the "Seventeen-Article Constitution" of Japan by **Shotoku Taishi** (shoh-TOH-koo ty-EE-shee; 573–621). In Japan, of course, Christianity was not even a factor—but the belief systems of Buddhism and Confucianism, both imported from China, along with Japan's native Shinto religion, were.

The Japanese constitution represents a level of agreement between religion and politics that would have been practically impossible in the West, where even in the Middle Ages people felt much more free to hold their own opinions. This harmony was possible precisely because there was even less separation of church and state in Japan than there was in medieval Europe.

Gregory of Tours

Excerpt from History of the Franks
Published in *Readings in European History,* **1905**

When one studies the relationship between medieval European kingdoms and the Catholic Church, it is hard to imagine a time when the kings of Western Europe were not Christians, or at least not Catholic. But before the time of Clovis (c. 466–511; ruled 481–511), tribal kings accepted a number of different faiths. Hence Clovis's conversion to Christianity in 496, an event recorded by Gregory of Tours (TOOR; 538–594) in his *History of the Franks,* was an event of key importance.

In Clovis's time, the Western Roman Empire lay in ruins, and a variety of invading tribes ruled most of Western Europe. Among these tribes were the Franks, Clovis's people, who eventually gave their name to the region they occupied: France. They were far from the most powerful among the tribes of Europe, which included the Visigoths who controlled Spain, or the Ostrogoths in control of Italy. Many of these groups had converted to Christianity, but to a form of the Christian faith that had been declared *heresy* (HAIR-uh-see)—that is, a doctrine that went against the Christian faith—by the pope, leader of the Catholic Church. This

"And seizing his ax, he cast it on the ground. And when the soldier had bent a little to pick it up the king raised his hands and crushed his head with his own ax. 'Thus,' he said, 'didst thou to the vase at Soissons.'"

Gregory of Tours

Gregory of Tours was among the most important historians of the early medieval period in Western Europe. Born Georgius Florentius (JOHR-jus flohr-EN-shus), he lived most of his life in what is now France. During Gregory's time, the Franks—who later gave their name to the entire country—controlled the region, and by then they had converted to Christianity. Gregory's *History of the Franks* records how this conversion came about, in the time of Clovis (ruled 481–511), the first important Frankish king.

Gregory became bishop, or the leading church official, for the city of Tours in 573. For many years, he was involved in a dispute with Clovis's grandson Chilperic (KIL-pur-ik; ruled 561–84), a harsh king whose reign was characterized by war, high taxes, and conflict with the clergy, or priests. Comparing him not only to one of the cruelest emperors of ancient Rome, but also to the king who had tried to kill the baby Jesus, Gregory called Chilperic "the Nero and Herod of our time."

In addition to *History of the Franks*, Gregory wrote a book on the lives of the saints, and one on famous miracles—both popular topics for medieval historians. After his death, he was canonized, or named as a saint.

heresy was called Arianism, and it taught that Christ was not God, but simply another one of God's creations.

The Franks, meanwhile, had not converted to Christianity; instead, they remained *pagan,* worshiping a variety of gods, most of whom represented forces of nature. In addition to their traditional deities or gods, they had also adopted Roman deities, such as Jupiter and Venus. But in most other regards they remained thoroughly un-Roman; thus they, along with a number of other tribes, were regarded as barbarians, or uncivilized. Gregory's account of what Clovis did to a rebellious soldier in Soissons (swah-SAWn), a town in northern France, illustrates their uncivilized behavior.

About seven years after the incident at Soissons, in 493, Clovis married Clotilde (kluh-TIL-duh; sometimes spelled Clotilda; c. 470–545), a princess from eastern France. Her people, the Burgundians, were Christians, and Clotilde herself was a devout Christian. As Gregory recounted, she continually urged her husband to accept the new faith, but he refused—until the time came when he needed God's blessing in a battle against a group of tribes called the Alemanni (al-uh-MAHN-ee).

Things to remember while reading the excerpt from *History of the Franks*

- The two events described by Gregory of Tours took place about ten years apart: the incident of the vase at Soissons in 486, and Clovis's conversion in 496. In the meantime, Clovis married Clotilde, a Christian princess who soon gave him a son. Despite the fact that he had rejected Christianity himself, Clovis allowed her to have the infant baptized in a Christian church—and when the boy died, the king took this as a bad sign from the gods. They had another son, Chlodomir (KLOH-doh-mur), and again Clotilde arranged to have him baptized. This son, too, fell ill, and Clovis told her that Chlodomir would die as well; but according to Gregory, "his mother prayed, and by God's will the child recovered." Soon after the recovery of Chlodomir, Clovis converted to Christianity.

- Based on Gregory's account, it appears that long before his conversion, Clovis respected Christian leaders. Thus he sent back word to the bishop who requested that he return his vase that "... I will do what the bishop desires." This respect may have been the result of his wife's influence; on the other hand, "barbarian" kings were often noted for the admiration they had for religious figures—regardless of the religion.

- The priest who formally led Clovis to accept Christianity was Remigius (ruh-MEE-gee-us), bishop or leading church official for the town of Reims (RAM; also Rheims), which is in northern France.

- Christian baptism symbolizes Christ's death and rebirth: by being immersed in water and rising again, a believer symbolically ends one life and begins another. It is an important sacrament, or religious ceremony, though in Clovis's case the event became a particularly large celebration: he was king, and as a result of his conversion, his kingdom was converting as well. Though Gregory, using language taken from the Bible, wrote that "the power of

Pillaged: Looted or robbed.

Idolatry: Worshiping a statue of a god; Gregory was referring to Clovis's belief in the old pagan gods.

Borne: Carried.

Bishop: A figure in the Christian church assigned to oversee priests and believers in a given city or region.

Vessels: Vases.

Lot: Lottery or drawing.

Booty: Loot or spoils of war.

Valiant: Brave.

Discerning: Wise or thoughtful.

Impetuous: Overly quick to take action.

Aloft: Into the air.

Just: Fair.

Stupefied: Speechless with amazement.

Cherished a hidden wound: In other words, held a grudge.

Breast: Heart.

Campus Martius: Military base.

Show their arms in brilliant array: In other words, the army was to appear dressed for battle, with all their weapons in order, for a review by the king.

God went before" Clovis, who gained his subject's support for the conversion to Christianity, it is doubtful his subjects had much choice in the matter. Clovis was a powerful and severe man—the same king who had earlier crushed a rebellious soldier's head.

Excerpt from History of the Franks

*... At this time [A.D. 486] the army of Clovis **pillaged** many churches, for he was still sunk in the errors of **idolatry**. The soldiers had **borne** away from a church, with all the other ornaments of the holy ministry, a vase of marvelous size and beauty. The **bishop** of this church sent messengers to the king, begging that if the church might not recover any other of the holy **vessels**, at least this one might be restored. The king, bearing these things, replied to the messenger: "Follow thou us to Soissons, for there all things that have been acquired are to be divided. If the **lot** shall give me this vase, I will do what the bishop desires."*

*When he had reached Soissons, and all the **booty** had been placed in the midst of the army, the king pointed to this vase, and said: "I ask you, O most **valiant** warriors, not to refuse to me the vase in addition to my rightful part." Those of **discerning** mind among his men answered, "O glorious king, all things which we see are thine, and we ourselves are subject to thy power; now do what seems pleasing to thee, for none is strong enough to resist thee." When they had thus spoken one of the soldiers, **impetuous**, envious, and vain, raised his battle-axe **aloft** and crushed the vase with it, crying, "Thou shalt receive nothing of this unless a **just** lot give it to thee." At this all were **stupefied**.*

*The king bore his injury with the calmness of patience, and when he had received the crushed vase he gave it to the bishop's messenger, but he **cherished a hidden wound** in his **breast**. When a year had passed he ordered the whole army to come fully equipped to the **Campus Martius** and **show their arms in brilliant array**. But when he had reviewed them all he came to the breaker of the vase, and said to him, "No one bears his arms so clumsily as thou; for neither thy spear, nor thy sword, nor thy ax is ready for use." And seizing his ax, he cast it on the ground. And* when the soldier had bent a little to pick it up the king raised his hands and crushed his head with his own ax. "Thus," he said, "didst thou to the vase at Soissons."

... The queen unceasingly urged the king to acknowledge the true God, and forsake idols. But he could not **in any wise** be brought to believe until a war broke out with the Alemanni. Then he was by necessity compelled to confess what he had before willfully denied.

It happened that the two armies were in battle and there was great slaughter. Clovis' army was near to utter destruction. He saw the danger; his heart was stirred; he was moved to tears, and he raised his eyes to heaven, saying, "Jesus Christ, whom Clotilde declares to be the son of the living God, who it is said givest aid to the oppressed and victory to those who put their hope in thee, I beseech the glory of thy aid. If thou shalt grant me victory over these enemies and I test that power which people **consecrated** to thy name say they have proved concerning thee, I will believe in thee and be **baptized** in thy name. For I have called upon my gods, but, as I have proved, they are far removed from my aid. So I believe that they have no power, for they do not **succor** those who serve them. Now I call upon thee, and I long to believe in thee—all the more that [I] may escape my enemies."

When he had said these things, the Alemanni turned their backs and began to flee. When they saw that their king was killed, they submitted to the sway of Clovis, saying: "We wish that no more people should perish. Now we are thine." When the king had forbidden further war, and praised his soldiers, he told the queen how he had won the victory by calling on the name of Christ.

Then the queen sent to the blessed Remigius, bishop of the city of Rheims, praying him to bring to the king the gospel of salvation. The priest, little by little and secretly, led him to believe in the true

A medieval manuscript illustration of the baptism of Clovis. *Reproduced by permission of the Corbis Corporation.*

In any wise: By any means.

Consecrated: Committed.

Baptized: Lowered into water as a symbol of death and rebirth.

Succor: Aid.

Clotilde

The story of Clovis's conversion is not merely a tale of men; behind the scenes was a woman, his wife Clotilde, or Clotilda. She was a princess of the Burgundians, a group who settled in eastern France and gave their name to that region. Unlike the early Franks, the Burgundians accepted Christianity, and Clotilde's father Chilperic arranged to have her educated in the Christian faith.

In 493, when she was twenty-three years old, Clotilde married the Frankish king Clovis, who was not a Christian. She continually urged him to convert, and finally, in 496, Clovis accepted the new religion. Along with him, his armies and his subjects converted as well; thus Clotilde may be considered the woman who brought Christianity to France.

After Clovis died in 511, Clotilde retired to a monastery, a secluded place for people who have taken religious vows. There she spent the remaining thirty-four years of her life, dying at age seventy-five—an impressive achievement at a time when people seldom expected to live past the age of thirty.

Mortal: Subject to death, or capable of dying; the opposite of mortal is immortal.

Font: A large vessel in which people are baptized.

Embroidered hangings: Sewn banners and tapestries, or brightly colored cloths often depicting various scenes.

Adorned: Decorated.

Balsam: An oily substance with a sweet smell.

Omnipotent: All-powerful.

Trinity: The three persons of the Christian God: Father, Son, and Holy Spirit.

Anointed: To have oil poured on one's head as a symbol of commitment to Christ.

God, maker of heaven and earth, and to forsake idols, which could not help him nor anybody else.

But the king said: "Willingly will I hear thee, O father; but one thing is in the way—that the people who follow me are not content to leave their gods. I will go and speak to them according to thy word."

When be came among them, the power of God went before him, and before he had spoken all the people cried out together: "We cast off **mortal** gods, O righteous king, and we are ready to follow the God whom Remigius tells us is immortal."

These things were told to the bishop. He was filled with joy, and ordered the **font** to be prepared. The streets were shaded with **embroidered hangings**; the churches were **adorned** with white tapestries, the baptistery was set in order, the odor of **balsam** spread around, candles gleamed, and all the temple of the baptistery was filled with divine odor.... Then the king confessed the God **omnipotent** in the **Trinity**, and was baptized in the name of the Father, and of the Son, and of the Holy Ghost, and was **anointed** with the sacred **chrism** with the sign of the cross of Christ. Of his army there were baptized more than three thousand.

What happened next ...

Perhaps Clovis converted to Christianity because of his victory over the Alemanni, perhaps due to the influence of his wife—or perhaps because he recognized the political advantages that would come from conversion. His adoption of mainstream Christianity, as opposed to the Arian heresy, meant that Clovis was the only tribal king to receive the blessing of the Church, which would prove a powerful ally in times to come. As to whether his adoption of the Christian faith actually made the harsh Clovis a gentler man, not even Gregory of Tours could supply much evidence to suggest that it had.

Clovis belonged to the Merovingian (mair-oh-VIN-jee-un) dynasty or ruling house, and his reign marked the beginning of what historians refer to as the Merovingian Age (481–751). A series of military victories won Clovis control over a region larger than modern-day France, but his conquests did not outlast him by very long. At his death, he divided his lands between his sons (Chlodomir among them), and in the years that followed, the kingdom began to fall apart as his various descendants fought for control. Eventually power fell into the hands of palace officials called majordomos ("mayors of the palace"), of whom the most notable was Charles Martel (c. 688–741). Charles's son Pepin III (c. 714–768) founded the Carolingian dynasty (kayr-uh-LINJ-ee-un), destined to produce one of the medieval period's greatest rulers, Charlemagne (SHAHR-luh-main; 742–814; ruled 768–814).

Jewelry from the time of the Merovingian Age (481–751); Clovis ruled at the beginning of this dynasty. *Reproduced by permission of the Corbis Corporation.*

Chrism: Special oil used in churches for events such as baptism.

The strong relationship between Church and state established by Clovis was a lasting one. In 800, the pope would crown Charlemagne "Emperor of the Romans," and eventually this title would come to symbolize leadership over much of Europe in the form of the Holy Roman Empire.

Did you know ...

- Long after her death, a number of romantic legends concerning Clotilde, the queen who brought Christianity to France, spread throughout Western Europe.

- The most popular name among French kings was Louis (LOO-ee), a form of Clovis and thus a tribute to the fifth-century king who virtually established the nation of France. In 1789, some 1,400 years after Clovis, Louis XVI was overthrown by the French Revolution, but from 1814 to 1824, his brother reigned as Louis XVIII.

- Not all Frankish names are as well remembered as that of Clovis: names such as Clotilde, Chlodomir, and Chilperic sound unattractive to most modern people. Chilperic was the name not only of Clotilde's father, but of Clovis's and Clotilde's grandson. Comprising a list of further unusual names: Chilperic's wives and lovers included Fredegund and Galswintha. Chilperic married Galswintha because he was jealous of his brother, who had married her sister Brunhilda.

For More Information

Books

Dijkstra, Henk, editor. *History of the Ancient and Medieval World,* Volume 8: *Christianity and Islam.* New York: Marshall Cavendish, 1996.

Dijkstra, Henk, editor. *History of the Ancient and Medieval World,* Volume 9: *The Middle Ages.* New York: Marshall Cavendish, 1996.

Robinson, J. H. *Readings in European History,* Boston: Ginn, 1905.

Severy, Merle, editor. *The Age of Chivalry.* Washington, D.C.: National Geographic Society, 1969.

Web Sites

"The Franks." [Online] Available http://www.btinternet.com/~mark.furnival/franks.htm (last accessed July 28, 2000).

"Medieval Sourcebook: Gregory of Tours: On Clovis." *Medieval Sourcebook.* [Online] Available http://www.fordham.edu/halsall/source/gregtours1.html (last accessed July 28, 2000).

Shotoku Taishi

"Seventeen-Article Constitution"

Published in *Nihongi: Chronicles of Japan from Earliest Times to A.D. 697*, 1896

Though Japan had been inhabited for thousands of years, it first emerged as a unified nation under the leadership of the Yamato (yuh-MAH-toh; "imperial") family in the Kofun period (koh-FUN; 250–552). It is likely that these early Japanese were heavily influenced by visitors from China, and from the 300s onward, the country welcomed a steady stream of Chinese and Korean immigrants.

During the Asuka period (552–645), the royal court in Korea introduced the leaders of Japan to a new religion, Buddhism (BÜD-izm). This sparked a conflict among the Japanese ruling classes, many of whom still embraced Japan's traditional religion, Shinto ("way of the gods"). Leading the movement for the acceptance of Buddhism was the Soga clan, whose most powerful member was Prince Shotoku Taishi (shoh-TOH-koo ty-EE-shee; 573–621).

"Sincerely reverence the three treasures. The three treasures: the Buddha, the Law, and the Priesthood, are the ... supreme objects of faith in all countries. What man in what age can fail to reverence this law?"

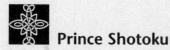

Prince Shotoku

Shotoku Taishi was among the most important figures in early Japanese history. In fact, it was he who gave the country its name; and his "Seventeen-Article Constitution," adopted in 604, gave a formal structure to the Japanese imperial government. Shotoku also helped establish the principles of Buddhism and Confucianism in Japan, and along with Japan's native Shinto religion, these continued to govern Japanese society through the twentieth century.

Because of his legendary status, it is hard to separate fact from myth concerning Shotoku's early life. Apparently he was born in the city of Asuka, then Japan's capital, but little else is known about his career until his early twenties. Shotoku belonged to the highly influential Soga family, who were the real power behind the Japanese emperors, and in 593 his aunt assumed the throne as the empress Suiko (soo-EE-koh; ruled 592–628). Shotoku became her regent, meaning that he ruled the country on her behalf.

During the next three decades, Shotoku engaged in a number of significant undertakings. Not only did he help to solidify the influence of Buddhism in Japanese society, he built a number of temples around the country, along with an extensive system of highways. In addition to his constitution, he introduced a new system of twelve court ranks based on another belief system which, like Buddhism, had been imported from China: Confucianism. He also instituted reforms in areas such as social welfare (caring for the poor) and land reclamation, the raising of land formerly covered by water. After his death, Japanese Buddhists began to view him as a Buddhist saint.

In 604, Shotoku issued his "Seventeen-Article Constitution." The document gave the central government enormous powers, and encouraged citizens to know their place in society. In addition to a number of clearly expressed Buddhist principles, the constitution also reflected the influence of Confucianism (kun-FYOO-shun-izm), another way of thought that had been introduced from mainland Asia.

Things to remember while reading the "Seventeen-Article Constitution"

- A constitution is a written document containing the laws of a nation, and is typically divided into articles, or individual statements of principle. For instance, the U.S. Constitution, adopted in 1787, has seven articles, addressing matters such as the roles of the president, Congress, and judges.

• Shotoku's constitution reflects a number of belief systems, most notably Buddhism and Confucianism. In Article 2, for instance, he mentions "the three treasures: the Buddha, the Law, and the Priesthood"—three key elements of the Buddhist faith. Buddhism originated in India with Siddhartha Gautama (si-DAR-tuh GOW-tuh-muh; c. 563–c. 483 B.C.), the Buddha or "enlightened one," who taught that the key to enlightenment or heightened understanding was to forsake one's personal desires. Later the religion spread to China and the rest of East Asia, where it took hold to a greater extent than it had in India.

A statue of Buddha. Shotoku Taishi's "Seventeen-Article Constitution" expresses several principles of Buddhism. *Reproduced by permission of the Corbis Corporation.*

• Another strong element in the constitution is Confucianism, based on the teachings of Confucius (551–479 B.C.). A belief system that stresses on social order and fulfilling one's mission in society, Confucianism had long held sway in China, and would continue to do so until the beginning of the twentieth century. An example of Confucianism in Shotoku's constitution is the statement in Article 1: "But when those above are harmonious and those below are friendly, and there is concord in the discussion of business, right views of things spontaneously gain acceptance." What this means, in other words, is that everyone should fulfill their role and work in agreement with one another.

• Also notable in the constitution are certain Chinese ideas. Among these is the comparison of the king to Heaven, and the people to Earth, in Article 3. The Chinese believed that the power of their emperors came from the "Mandate of Heaven," meaning the favor of the gods, and the Japanese also adopted this belief regarding their own leaders.

"Seventeen-Article Constitution"

*1. **Harmony** is to be valued, and an avoidance of **wanton** opposition to be honored. All men are influenced by **class-feelings**, and there are few who are intelligent. Hence there are some who disobey their lords and fathers, or who maintain **feuds** with the neighboring villages. But when those above are harmonious and those below are friendly, and there is **concord** in the discussion of business, right views of things **spontaneously** gain acceptance. Then what is there which cannot be accomplished!*

*2. Sincerely **reverence** the three treasures. The three treasures: the Buddha, the Law, and the Priesthood, are the ... supreme objects of faith in all countries. What man in what age can fail to reverence this law? Few men are utterly bad. They may be taught to follow it. But if they do not go to the three treasures, how shall their crookedness be made straight?*

*3. When you receive the Imperial commands, fail not **scrupulously** to obey them. The lord is Heaven, the **vassal** is Earth. Heaven overspreads, and Earth upbears. When this is so, the four seasons follow their due course, and the powers of Nature **obtain their efficacy**. If the Earth attempted to overspread, Heaven would simply fall in ruin. Therefore is it that when the lord speaks, the vassal listens; when the superior acts, the inferior yields **compliance**. Consequently when you receive the Imperial commands, fail not to carry them out scrupulously. Let there be a want of care in this matter, and ruin is the natural consequence.*

*4. The **Ministers and functionaries** should make **decorous** behavior their leading principle, for the leading principle of the government of the people consists in decorous behavior. If the superiors do not behave with **decorum**, the inferiors are disorderly: if inferiors are **wanting in** proper behavior, there must necessarily be offenses. Therefore it is that when lord and vassal behave with **propriety**, the distinc-*

Harmony: Agreement.

Wanton: Unjustified and cruel.

Class-feelings: Awareness of one's place in society, along with a desire to get ahead.

Feuds: Conflicts.

Concord: Unity.

Spontaneously: Automatically.

Reverence: Honor.

Scrupulously: Righteously.

Vassal: Someone who is subject to a lord or king.

Obtain their efficacy: Function at their best.

Compliance: Agreement.

Ministers and functionaries: Respectively, higher and lower government officials.

Decorous: Proper.

Decorum: Appropriateness.

Wanting in: Lacking.

Propriety: Correctness.

tions of rank are not confused: when the people behave with propriety, the Government of the **Commonwealth** proceeds of itself....

6. **Chastise** that which is evil and encourage that which is good. This was the excellent rule of **antiquity**. Conceal not, therefore, the good qualities of others, and fail not to correct that which is wrong when you see it. Flatterers and **deceivers** are a sharp weapon for the overthrow of **the State**, and a pointed sword for the destruction of the people. **Sycophants** are also fond, when they meet, of speaking at length to their superiors on the errors of their inferiors; to their inferiors, they **censure** the faults of their superiors. Men of this kind are all wanting in **fidelity** to their lord, and in **benevolence** toward the people. From such an origin great civil disturbances arise.

7. Let every man have his own charge, and let not the **spheres of duty** be confused. When wise men are entrusted with office, the sound of praise arises. If **unprincipled** men hold office, disasters and **tumults** are multiplied. In this world, few are born with knowledge: wisdom is the product of **earnest** meditation. In all things, whether great or small, find the right man, and they [the people] will surely be well managed: on all occasions, be they urgent or the reverse, meet but with a wise man, and they will of themselves be **amenable**. In this way will the State be lasting and the Temples of the Earth and of Grain will be free from danger. Therefore did the wise **sovereigns** of antiquity seek the man to fill the office, and not the office for the sake of the man....

10. Let us cease from wrath, and refrain from angry looks. Nor let us be resentful when others differ from us. For all men have hearts, and each heart has its own leanings. Their right is our wrong, and our right is their wrong. We are not unquestionably **sages**, nor are they unquestionably fools. Both of us are simply ordinary men. How can any one lay down a rule by which to distinguish right from wrong? For we are all, one with another, wise and foolish, like a ring which has no end. Therefore, although others give way to anger, let us on the contrary dread our own faults, and though we alone may be in the right, let us follow the multitude and act like men....

11. Give clear appreciation to merit and **demerit**, and deal out to each its sure reward or punishment. In these days, reward does not attend upon merit, nor punishment upon crime. You high functionaries who have charge of public affairs, let it be your task to make clear rewards and punishments....

Commonwealth: A nation or state.

Chastise: Rebuke or scold.

Antiquity: Ancient or earlier times.

Deceivers: Liars.

The State: The government.

Sycophants: Self-serving flatterers.

Censure: Condemn.

Fidelity: Loyalty.

Benevolence: Good will.

Spheres of duty: Areas of authority.

Unprincipled: Dishonest.

Tumults: Troubles.

Earnest: Sincere and serious.

Amenable: Agreeable.

Sovereigns: Kings and other leaders.

Sages: Wise men.

Demerit: Something lacking in merit, or worth.

*15. To turn away from that which is private, and to set our faces toward that which is public—this is the path of a Minister. Now if a man is influenced by private motives, he will assuredly feel resentments, and if he is influenced by resentful feelings, he will assuredly fail to act harmoniously with others. If he fails to act harmoniously with others, he will assuredly sacrifice the public interests to his private feelings. When resentment arises, it interferes with order, and is **subversive of** law....*

16. Let the people be employed [in labor on public works projects] at seasonable times. This is an ancient and excellent rule. Let them be employed, therefore, in the winter months, when they are at leisure [when there are no crops to plant or harvest]. But from Spring to Autumn, when they are engaged in agriculture or with the mulberry trees, the people should not be so employed. For if they do not attend to agriculture, what will they have to eat? If they do not attend the mulberry trees, what will they do for clothing?

*17. Decisions on important matters should not be made by one person alone.... They should be discussed with many. But small matters are of less consequence. It is unnecessary to consult a number of people. It is only in the case of the discussion of weighty affairs, when there is a suspicion that they may **miscarry**, that one should arrange matters in **concert** with others, so as to arrive at the right conclusion.*

Subversive of: Having a weakening effect on.

Miscarry: Go wrong.

Concert (adj.): Agreement.

What happened next ...

The power of the Soga clan weakened after the death of Shotoku in 622, and in 645 Crown Prince Nakano Oe (OH-ee; 626–671) and Nakatomi Kamatari (614–669) joined forces to overthrow the government. Later the prince became the Emperor Tenchi, and Kamatari's family became known as Fujiwara, a clan that would later dominate the imperial family.

During the Hakuh period (645–710), the Japanese fully accepted an idea already evident in the Seventeen-Article Constitution: that the emperor was a god. This concept would continue to hold sway, even though the emperors themselves did not always possess real political power. Tenchi was a strong leader, introducing a number of reforms modeled on those of China's T'ang dynasty (DAHNG; 618–907), but later emperors tended to be dominated by powerful families such as the Fujiwara.

During the Heian period (hay-YAHN; 794–1185), the Japanese imperial court became increasingly separated from the countryside. Rural areas of Japan functioned as independent kingdoms, further weakening the power of the emperors. Years of civil war and conflict followed, and it would be many centuries before the emperors again asserted their power.

Did you know ...

- Shotoku gave Japan its name, Nippon or Nihon. In 607, he sent a group of officials to China, and they came bearing a message which began "The emperor of the country where the sun rises addresses a letter to the emperor of the country where the sun sets." The Chinese began to call the country to the east *Jihpen,* meaning "origins of the sun." Later the Italian traveler Marco Polo, who visited China in the 1200s, brought this name back with him to Europe, where it became "Japan."

- Among the many buildings erected under Shotoku's leadership was a Buddhist temple at Horyuji (HOHR-yoo-jee), built in 607. It is the world's oldest wooden structure.

- The writings of Shotoku may have formed the basis for the *Nihon shoki,* Japan's first book of history, the various stories and legends of which were compiled in 720.

For More Information

Books

Aston, W. G., translator. *Nihongi: Chronicles of Japan from Earliest Times to A.D. 697,* Volume 2. London: Keegan and Co., 1896.

Dijkstra, Henk, editor. *History of the Ancient and Medieval World,* Volume 11: *Empires of the Ancient World.* New York: Marshall Cavendish, 1996.

Pilbeam, Mavis. *Japan: 5000 B.C.–Today.* New York: Franklin Watts, 1988.

Web Sites

Internet East Asian History Sourcebook. [Online] Available http://www.fordham.edu/halsall/eastasia/eastasiasbook.html (last accessed July 28, 2000).

"The Japanese Constitution." [Online] Available http://www.wsu.edu:8080/~dee/ANCJAPAN/CONST.HTM (last accessed July 28, 2000).

Emperor Henry IV

"Letter to Gregory VII," January 24, 1076
Published in *Select Historical Documents of the Middle Ages*, 1910

Pope Gregory VII

"First Deposition and Banning of Henry IV," February 22, 1076
Published in *Select Historical Documents of the Middle Ages*, 1910

During the early part of the Middle Ages, popes—that is, the spiritual and political leaders of the Catholic Church—enjoyed good relations with kings in Western Europe. This had been the case since the time of Clovis, king of the Franks, and the strong relationship became stronger in 800, when Pope Leo III crowned the Frankish king Charlemagne (SHAHR-luh-main; ruled 768–814) as "Emperor of the Romans."

That title suggested that the Western Roman Empire, which had died out in 476, would gain a new life through the combined powers of Church and state. This new Roman Empire, however, remained a vaguely defined political unit. Eventually it was called the Holy Roman Empire, and as such it brought together a number of smaller states within what is now Germany and surrounding countries. Holy Roman emperors, however, always had to struggle to maintain their power, facing conflict on the one hand from various princes and dukes within their kingdoms, and on the other hand from the popes in Rome.

"Henry, king not through usurpation but through the holy ordination of God, to Hildebrand [Gregory], at present not pope but false monk."

From "Letter to Gregory VII"

Henry IV

Henry IV (1050–1106) became king of Germany in 1056, when he was only six years old. Traditionally, kings of Germany also became Holy Roman Emperor, and thus Henry's reign as emperor dates from 1056 as well, but he was not crowned until 1084. Until he came of age, Henry's mother Agnes ruled in his place as regent; by 1066, however, sixteen-year-old Henry was in charge.

Henry's reign was marked by struggle, first with nobles—rulers within his kingdom who had inherited title and lands, but held less power than the king—from the German region of Saxony. From 1073 to 1088, he fought a long war with the Saxon nobles, but in the midst of this he became caught up in a conflict with an even more powerful figure: the pope.

The years from 1076 to 1084 were hard ones for Henry. First he was excommunicated, or removed from the Church, by Pope Gregory VII. Then, in 1077, he was allowed to return to the Church, but three years later he was defeated in war by the Duke of Swabia, a region in Germany. Gregory excommunicated him again in 1080, but in 1084 Henry had Gregory removed from power.

Eventually Henry had to face more conflict, this time from within his own family. In 1093, his sons rebelled against him, and in 1105 one of them had him imprisoned. Henry escaped, but died soon afterward.

The conflict with the papacy (PAY-puh-see), or the office of the pope, was particularly significant, because both popes and emperors claimed to be the leaders of Western Europe. During the latter part of the 1000s, this struggle came to a head in the Investiture Controversy. "Controversy" is another term for conflict, and "investiture" referred to the power of Holy Roman emperors to invest or appoint local church leaders. Chief among these church leaders were bishops, who had authority over all the priests and believers in a given city or region.

On December 8, 1075, Pope Gregory VII (ruled 1073–85), also known as Hildebrand, sent orders to Emperor Henry IV (ruled 1056–1106) that he should stop appointing bishops. Henry responded with a blistering letter, and Gregory in turn issued an order telling Henry's subjects that they were no longer required to obey him.

Things to remember while reading the "Letter to Gregory VII" and the "First Deposition and Banning of Henry IV"

- Both Henry's letter to Gregory, and Gregory's orders deposing Henry (that is, removing him from power) rely heavily on claims to rightful spiritual authority, and both men used passages from the Bible to back up their claims. Henry referred to the Old Testament practice of anointing, whereby a prophet of God poured oil over the head of someone God had chosen to be leader. Several passages in the Bible contain warnings to "touch not God's anointed." In the New Testament, both Jesus and the Apostle Paul commanded believers to submit to the authority of lawfully chosen kings, and though as Henry noted, a number of early Church leaders had said that Christians were not required to follow ungodly leaders, he claimed that he was not one of these.

- In his orders condemning Henry, Gregory addressed St. Peter, or the Apostle Peter, who, according to Catholic tradition, was the first pope. Thus Gregory was in effect embracing what he believed was an unbroken line of authority that went back more than 1,000 years. This belief was based on a statement of Christ in the New Testament Book of Matthew, Chapter 16: speaking to Peter, whose name means "rock" in Greek, Jesus said that "upon this rock I will build my church." In the same passage, Christ also said that "whatsover is bound on earth will be bound in heaven, and whatsover is loosed on earth will be loosed in heaven," also interpreted by Catholics as a command giving authority to Peter and those who followed him.

- Henry mentioned two figures from the earlier history of the Church. Julian the Apostate (ruled 361–63) was a Roman emperor who rejected Christianity and tried to return Romans to the worship of their old gods such as Jupiter—hence the title of Apostate (uh-PAHS-tayt), meaning "betrayer." St. Gregory was Pope Gregory I, or Gregory the Great (ruled 590–604), one of the most admired leaders of the early Church. The statement quoted by Gregory can be interpreted to mean that when a ruler gains too much power, he is filled with pride and does not submit to God's authority—as Henry claimed the current Pope Gregory was doing.

- Henry used the "royal we": instead of referring to himself in the first-person singular (*I, me, mine*), he spoke of himself in the plural. This was a tradition among kings and other people in authority, whose use of the plural meant that they saw themselves as representing their entire kingdom. When Henry wrote that he was "unworthy to be among the anointed," this was merely an attempt to appear modest: if he had really considered himself unworthy, he would not have challenged Gregory's authority.

"Letter to Gregory VII," January 24, 1076

*Henry, king not through **usurpation** but through the holy **ordination** of God, to Hildebrand, at present not pope but false monk.*

*Such greeting as this hast thou merited through thy disturbances, inasmuch as there is no **grade** in the church which thou hast **omitted** to make a partaker not of honour but of confusion, not of **benediction** but of **malediction**. For, to mention few and **especial** cases out of many, not only hast thou not feared to lay hands upon the rulers of the holy church, the anointed of the Lord—the **archbishops**, namely, bishops and priests—but thou hast **trodden** them under foot like slaves ignorant of what their master is doing. Thou hast won favour from the common herd by crushing them; thou hast looked upon all of them as knowing nothing, upon thy sole self, moreover, as knowing all things. This knowledge, however, thou hast used not for **edification** but for destruction; so that with reason we believe that St. Gregory, whose name thou has usurped for thyself, was prophesying concerning thee when he said: "The pride of him who is in power increases the more, the greater the number of those subject to him; and he thinks that he himself can do more than all." And we, indeed, have endured all this, being eager to guard the honour of the **apostolic see**; thou, however, has understood our humility to be fear, and hast not, accordingly, **shunned** to rise up against the royal power conferred upon us by God, daring to threaten to **divest** us of it. As if we had received our kingdom from thee! As if the kingdom and the empire were in thine and not in God's hand! And this although our Lord Jesus Christ did call us to the kingdom, did not, however, call thee to the priesthood. For thou*

Usurpation: The act of seizing power unlawfully.

Ordination: The act of being lawfully placed in a position or office.

Grade: Office or position.

Omitted: In this context, failed.

Benediction: Blessing.

Malediction: A curse.

Especial: Specific.

Archbishops: The leading bishops (figures in the Christian church assigned to oversee priests and believers) in an area or nation.

Trodden: Trampled.

Edification: Building up.

Apostolic see: The papacy, or office of the pope.

Shunned: In this context, failed.

Divest: Remove.

has ascended by the following steps. By **wiles**, namely, which the profession of monk abhors, thou has achieved money; by money, favour; by the sword, **the throne of peace**. And from the throne of peace thou hast disturbed peace, inasmuch as thou hast armed subjects against those in authority over them; inasmuch as thou, who wert not **called**, hast taught that our bishops called of God are to be despised; inasmuch as thou hast usurped for **laymen** and the ministry over their priests, allowing them to **depose** or condemn those whom they themselves had received as teachers from the hand of God through the laying on of hands of the bishops. On me also who, although unworthy to be among **the anointed**, have nevertheless been anointed to the kingdom, thou hast lain thy hand; me who as the tradition of the **holy Fathers** teaches, declaring that I am not to be deposed for any crime unless, which God forbid, I should have strayed from the faith—am subject to the judgment of God alone. For the wisdom of the holy fathers committed even Julian the **apostate** not to themselves, but to God alone, to be judged and to be deposed. For himself the true pope, Peter, also exclaims: "Fear God, honour the king." But thou who does not fear God, dost dishonour in me his appointed one. Wherefore St. Paul, **when he has not spared an angel of Heaven if he shall have preached otherwise**, has not excepted thee also who dost teach otherwise upon earth. For he says: "If any one, either I or an angel from Heaven, should preach a gospel other than that which has been preached to you, he shall be **damned**." Thou, therefore, damned by this curse and by the judgment of all our bishops and by our own, [should] descend and **relinquish** the apostolic chair which thou has usurped. Let another **ascend** the throne of St. Peter, who shall not practise violence under the cloak of religion, but shall teach the sound doctrine of St. Peter. I Henry, king by the grace of God, do say unto thee, together with all our bishops: Descend, descend, to be damned throughout the ages.

"First Deposition and Banning of Henry IV," February 22, 1076

O St. Peter, chief of the **apostles**, incline to us, I beg, thy holy ears, and hear me thy servant whom thou has nourished from infancy, and whom, until this day, thou hast freed from the hand of the wicked, who have hated and do hate me for my faithfulness to thee. Thou, and **my mistress the mother of God**, and thy brother St. Paul are witnesses for me among all the saints that thy holy Roman church **drew me to its helm against my will**; that I had no thought

Wiles: Tricks.

The throne of peace: The papacy.

Called: In other words, ordained or placed in office by proper authority.

Laymen: Ordinary believers, as opposed to priests and others within the Church itself.

Depose: Remove.

The anointed: Those chosen by God to fill a position of leadership.

Holy Fathers: Early Church leaders.

Apostate: Betrayer.

When he has not spared an angel of Heaven if he shall have preached otherwise: In other words, whose preaching has taken account of all special circumstances.

Damned: Condemned to hell.

Relinquish: Give up.

Ascend: Rise to.

Apostles: Religious figures sent out to teach, preach, and perform miracles.

My mistress the mother of God: The Virgin Mary.

Drew me to its helm against my will: In other words, "I became pope not because I wanted to, but because it was required of me."

of ascending thy chair through force, and that I would rather have ended my life as a **pilgrim** than, by **secular** means, to have seized thy throne for the sake of earthly glory. And therefore I believe it to be through thy grace and not through my own deeds that it has pleased and does please thee that the Christian people, who have been especially committed to thee, should obey me. And especially to me, as thy representative and by thy favour, has the power been granted by God of binding and loosing in Heaven and on earth. On the strength of this belief therefore, for the honour and security of thy church, in the name of Almighty God, Father, Son and Holy Ghost, I withdraw, through thy power and authority, from Henry the king, son of Henry the emperor, who has risen against thy church with unheard of **insolence**, the rule over the whole kingdom of the Germans and over Italy. And I **absolve** all Christians from the bonds of the oath which they have made or shall make to him; and I forbid any one to serve him as king. For it is fitting that he who **strives** to lessen the honour of thy church should himself lose the honour which belongs to him. And since he has **scorned** to obey as a Christian, and has not returned to God whom he had deserted—holding **intercourse** with **the excommunicated;** practising **manifold iniquities; spurning** my commands which, as thou dost bear witness, I issued to him for his own salvation; separating himself from thy church and striving to rend it—I bind him in thy stead with the chain of the **anathema.** And, leaning on thee, I so bind him that the people may know and have proof that thou art Peter, and above thy rock the Son of the living God hath built His church, and the gates of Hell shall not prevail against it.

What happened next ...

After Gregory excommunicated him, or removed him from the Church, Henry lost the support of his nobles. Therefore in January 1077, in a symbolic act of humility and submission, he appeared at the castle of Canossa (kuh-NAH-suh) in northern Italy, where the pope was staying, and waited barefoot outside in the snow for hours until the pope forgave him. By then Henry was caught up in a war with the Duke of Swabia, a region in Germany, and Gregory tried to help the

Pilgrim: Someone who journeys to holy places.

Secular: Nonspiritual.

Insolence: Impudence or rudeness.

Absolve: Excuse.

Strives: Works.

Scorned: Refused.

Intercourse: Communication.

The excommunicated: People who have been forced to leave the Church.

Manifold: Many.

Iniquities: Sins.

Spurning: Rejecting.

Anathema: Someone or something that is cursed and rejected.

Pope Gregory VII

Pope Gregory VII (c. 1020–1085) was born with the name Hildebrand, and thus he was sometimes referred to as Gregory VII Hildebrand. He spent his early career as a monk, a figure within the Church who forsakes the world in order to pursue a life of prayer and meditation. Soon, however, he became involved in Church leadership, serving first as chaplain to Pope Gregory VI from 1045 to 1047.

When Gregory VI was removed from power on charges of simony (accepting money to appoint people to offices within the Church) and sent away to Germany, Hildebrand went with him. In 1049, however, he returned to Rome to serve as advisor to Pope Leo IX, and during the next quarter-century he served in a number of important functions. Finally, in 1075 he was elected pope himself.

Seeking to assert the authority of the popes over political leaders, Gregory quickly issued an order against lay investiture (appointment of Church officials by laymen, or people who were not priests or Church leaders themselves). This aroused

Pope Gregory VII. *Reproduced by permission of Archive Photos, Inc.*

the anger of Emperor Henry IV, and the next decade was marked by an on-again, off-again struggle with Henry. Finally, in 1084, Henry removed Gregory from power. Gregory died a year later, but because the man who replaced him was judged an antipope (a false claimant to the title of pope), official Church history holds that Gregory remained rightful pope until his death.

two settle the dispute; but in 1080, the same year that the Duke of Swabia defeated Henry, Gregory again excommunicated the emperor.

Four years later, in 1084, Henry marched his troops into Rome and removed Gregory from power, replacing him with Clement III (c. 1025–1100), who was later judged by Church authorities as an antipope, or unlawful claimant on

the title of pope. Gregory died a year later, in exile under the protection of the Guiscard (gee-SKARD) family who controlled Sicily. Henry lived another twenty years, but he suffered a sad fate similar to that of Gregory: in 1105, one of his sons had him dethroned and imprisoned, and though he escaped, he died soon afterward.

Meanwhile the world moved on. A new pope, Urban II (ruled 1088–99), had inherited Gregory's enthusiasm for papal authority. He would launch the First Crusade (1095–99), a war to recapture the Holy Land, or Palestine, from the Muslims who controlled it. In so doing, he would greatly build up the power of the popes. For the next three centuries, the papacy would be the center of political authority in Western Europe.

Henry IV kneels before Matilda of Tuscany. Matilda was a powerful supporter of Henry's opponent, Pope Gregory VII. *Reproduced by permission of the Corbis Corporation.*

Did you know ...

- When Henry went to visit Gregory in the castle at Canossa and beg his forgiveness, he was dressed in a plain woolen shirt with bare feet as a symbol of his submission to the pope. Gregory made him wait outside in the snow—it was January—for three days. Later, the expression "going to Canossa" came to symbolize an act of humility before a leader.

- One of Gregory's most powerful supporters, and indeed one of the most significant female leaders of medieval Western Europe, was the princess Matilda of Tuscany (1046–1115), owner of the castle at Canossa. She waged a number of wars against Henry between 1080 and 1106.

- England had its own version of the Investiture Controversy, involving King William II (ruled 1087–1100) and Anselm of Canterbury (c. 1034–1109), one of the most important thinkers in medieval Europe. Later Anselm settled his differences with William's younger brother Henry I (ruled 1100–1135).

For More Information

Books

Dijkstra, Henk, editor. *History of the Ancient and Medieval World,* Volume 9: *The Middle Ages.* New York: Marshall Cavendish, 1996.

Hanawalt, Barbara A. *The Middle Ages: An Illustrated History.* New York: Oxford University Press, 1998.

Henderson, Ernest F., translator. *Select Historical Documents of the Middle Ages.* London: George Bell and Sons.

Jones, Terry and Alan Ereira. *Crusades.* New York: Facts on File, 1995.

Web Sites

Medieval Sourcebook: Empire and Papacy. [Online] Available http://www.fordham.edu/halsall/sbook1l.html (last accessed July 28, 2000).

Dante Alighieri

Excerpt from the **Divine Comedy**
Published in *The Divine Comedy of Dante Alighieri*, 1906

The poet Dante Alighieri (DAHN-tay al-eeg-YEER-ee; 1265–1321), usually referred to simply as Dante, is considered one of the greatest writers of all time—on a par with figures such as the Greek poet Homer (700s B.C.) or the English playwright and poet William Shakespeare (1564–1616). By far the most widely admired of Dante's works is the *Divine Comedy,* which is not a comedy in the traditional sense: here the term refers to the fact that the story, told in a series of 100 "chapters" called cantos, has a happy ending.

The term "divine" is a reference to God, an abiding presence in the narrative as the poet journeys into the depths of the Inferno or Hell, guided by the departed soul of the Roman poet Virgil (70–19 B.C.; sometimes rendered as Vergil or Virgilius). Later, Dante describes a journey into Purgatory, a place of punishment for people working out their salvation and earning their way into Heaven or Paradise. A journey through Heaven constitutes the final section of the *Divine Comedy.*

This vast work is so complex and rich in detail that it is hard to do it justice in just a few words (see box, "The *Di-*

"Beneath my head the others are dragged down / Who have preceded me in simony, / Flattened along the fissure of the rock."

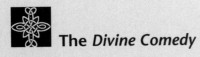

The *Divine Comedy*

Considered one of the world's great literary works, Dante's *Divine Comedy* is a long poem describing the author's journey into Hell, or the Inferno; then through the center of the Earth to Purgatory, a place of punishment for people working out their salvation; and finally, through the planets and stars into Heaven or Paradise.

Dante places the events of the *Divine Comedy* at Easter Weekend 1300, when he was—as he wrote in the open lines of Canto I—"in the middle of the journey of our life" (in other words, thirty-five years old). But the *Divine Comedy* is not meant to be understood as a literal story; rather, it is an allegory, or symbolic tale. Nor is it a comedy as that word is normally used: rather, the term "comedy" refers to the fact that after passing through great misfortune, the author is given a glimpse of the Heaven that awaits believers.

The *Divine Comedy* consists of 100 cantos, or chapters, which are in turn composed of verses. After an introductory canto in which Dante describes how he entered Hell through a darkened forest, each section comprises thirty-three cantos. In each place, Dante travels with a guide: in the Inferno, the Roman poet Virgil (70–19 B.C.), and in Purgatory and Paradise, his beloved Beatrice. The book is densely packed with references to people and events in Europe from ancient times through the early 1300s, and in order to enjoy it fully, a modern reader must consult extensive reference notes. It is a rewarding exercise, however, and anyone who reads the entire *Divine Comedy* comes away with an encyclopedic knowledge of the medieval world. Those fortunate enough to read it in Italian also have an opportunity to enjoy Dante's simple but beautiful language in the original.

vine Comedy"). The passage that follows is drawn from Canto XIX of the Inferno, where Dante witnesses the punishment of popes and other Church leaders guilty of simony—the buying and selling of offices within the Church. Their punishment is particularly gruesome: they have been shoved headfirst, one on top of another, into a bottomless hole in the ground. The newest arrival must suffer the burning of his feet; but when another simoniac (someone who practices simony) dies, the earlier ones will be pushed farther down, deeper into the earth. As Dante notes, this was like the means used to execute hired killers, who were placed headfirst in a pit, then covered with dirt until they suffocated.

Things to remember while reading the excerpt from the *Divine Comedy*

- The *Divine Comedy* is an example of allegory, a style of writing popular throughout the Middle Ages. In allegory, characters and events are meant to be understood as symbols: obviously Dante did not actually journey into Hell, but used it as a symbolic setting in which to address a number of earthly problems. In this passage, the issue addressed is simony, the buying and selling of church offices.

- The simoniac with whom Dante talks in this passage is supposed to be Pope Nicholas III (ruled 1277–80), who came from the Orsini family—a clan known as "the cubs of the she-bear." Later, Dante mentions Nicholas's "intrigue against Charles." This is a reference to Charles of Anjou (ahn-ZHOO), a leader against whom Nicholas supposedly joined in a conspiracy.

A scene of Hell from Dante's *Divine Comedy;* Satan watches from the background with his wings outspread. *Reproduced by permission of the Corbis Corporation.*

- Nicholas mistakes Dante for Pope Boniface VIII (BAHN-i-fus; ruled 1294–1303); but the events of the *Divine Comedy* were supposed to take place in 1300, three years before Boniface's death. After Boniface, Nicholas predicts, will come an even worse offender. This was a reference to Pope Clement V (ruled 1305–1314), who in 1309 moved his headquarters from Rome to Avignon (AV-in-yawn) in southern France as a symbol of his submission to the king of France. This in turn sparked one of the greatest crises in the history of the Catholic Church. Nicholas compares Clement to Jason, a high priest of Jerusalem during the 100s B.C. After bribing the local ruler in order to become high priest, Jason tried to force the Jews to adopt the Greek religion. These events are recorded in the Book of Maccabees (MAK-uh-beez), which appears in some Catholic versions of the Bible.

- Angered by the simoniacs, Dante asks if Jesus charged St. Peter money before he gave the famous disciple a symbolic set of keys to unlock the gates of heaven (Gospel of Matthew, chapter 16, verse 19). This was particularly significant because the popes viewed themselves as successors to Peter, and thus as holders of those keys as well. Judas Iscariot had been the disciples' treasurer, but after he betrayed Jesus and committed suicide, Matthew took his place—but again, as Dante notes, none of the other disciples tried to obtain silver and gold from him.

- Later, Dante refers to another disciple by title rather than name: "The Evangelist." An evangelist is someone who preaches the Christian gospel; however, "The Evangelist" refers to John, disciple of Jesus and author of the Book of Revelation. This section of the Bible describes the end of the world, and among other events it depicts is an unholy alliance between a wicked woman—"she who sitteth upon many waters"—with the kings of the world. Early Church leaders compared the wicked woman to Rome before that city accepted Christianity, but Dante used her as a symbol for the corrupted Church. He also mentioned a beast with seven heads and ten horns, described in Revelation.

- In the final lines of this passage, Dante referred to Constantine (KAHN-stun-teen; ruled 306–337), the first Roman emperor to accept Christianity. This led to the Christianization of Rome, but in the belief of Dante and many others, it also corrupted the Church by giving it political power. His mention of the "marriage dower"—that is, a dowry or the wealth a bride brings to her marriage—referred to the New Testament idea of the Church ("mother" in this verse) as the bride of Christ. Dante and other people in medieval times believed that Constantine had formally granted political power to the Church in a document known as the Donation of Constantine, which was later proven to be a forgery, or falsified document.

Excerpt from **The Divine Comedy**

... I saw upon the sides and on the bottom
*The **livid** stone with **perforations** filled,*
All of one size, and every one was round....

*Out of the mouth of each one there **protruded***
*The feet of a **transgressor,** and the legs*
Up to the calf, the rest within remained.

In all of them the soles were both on fire;
Wherefore the joints so violently quivered,
*They would have **snapped asunder withes and bands.***

*Even as the flame of **unctuous** things is **wont***
To move upon the outer surface only,
So likewise was it there from heel to point....

*"**Whoe'er** thou art, that standest upside down,*
*O **doleful** soul, implanted like a stake,"*
*To say began I, "if thou **canst,** speak out."*

*I stood even as the **friar** who is **confessing***
*The false assassin, who, when he is **fixed,***
__Recalls him,__ so that death may be delayed.

*And he cried out: "**Dost thou** stand there already,*
Dost thou stand there already, Boniface?
By many years the record lied to me.

*Art thou so early **satiate** with that wealth,*
For which thou didst not fear to take by fraud
*__The beautiful Lady,__ and then work her **woe**?"*

Livid: Red.

Perforations: Holes.

Protruded: Stuck out.

Transgressor: Offender or sinner.

Snapped asunder: Broken.

Withes and bands: Strong ropes.

Unctuous: Oily.

Wont: Inclined.

Whoe'er: Whoever.

Doleful: Miserable.

Canst: Can.

Friar: A preacher and teacher, as opposed to a priest, in the Catholic Church.

Confessing: Receiving confession from.

Fixed: Placed in the ground.

Recalls him: Asks him to come back.

Dost thou ...?: Do you?

Satiate: Satisfied.

The beautiful Lady: The Church.

Woe: Misfortune.

Such I became, as people are who stand,
Not comprehending what is answered them,
*As if **bemocked**, and know not how to answer.*

Then said Virgilius: "Say to him straightway,
'I am not he, I am not he thou thinkest.'"
*And I replied **as was imposed on me.***

***Whereat** the spirit writhed with both his feet,*
*Then, sighing, with a voice of **lamentation***
Said to me: "Then what wantest thou of me?

If who I am thou carest so much to know,
That thou on that account hast crossed the bank,
*Know that **I vested was with the great mantle**;*

And truly was I son of the She-bear,
So eager to advance the cubs, that wealth
Above, and here myself, I pocketed.

Beneath my head the others are dragged down
*Who have preceded me in **simony**,*
*Flattened along the **fissure** of the rock.*

Below there I shall likewise fall, whenever
That one shall come who I believed thou wast,
What time the sudden question I proposed.

But longer I my feet already toast,
And here have been in this way upside down,
Than he will planted stay with reddened feet;

For after him shall come of fouler deed
From tow'rds the west a Pastor without law,
Such as befits to cover him and me.

New Jason will he be, of whom we read
*In Maccabees; and as his king was **pliant**,*
So he who governs France shall be to this one."

I do not know if I were here too bold,
*That him I answered only in this **metre**:*
*"I **pray** thee tell me now how great a treasure*

Our Lord demanded of Saint Peter first,
Before he put the keys into his keeping?
Truly he nothing asked but 'Follow me.'

Nor Peter nor the rest asked of Matthias
*Silver or gold, when he by **lot** was chosen*

Unto the place the guilty soul had lost.

Therefore stay here, for thou art justly punished,
And keep safe guard o'er the ill-gotten money,
Which caused thee to be **valiant** against Charles.

And were it not that still forbids it me
The **reverence** for the keys **superlative**
Thou hadst in keeping in the **gladsome** life,

I would make use of words more **grievous** still;
Because your **avarice afflicts** the world,
Trampling the good and lifting the **depraved.**

The Evangelist you Pastors had in mind,
When she who sitteth upon many waters
To fornicate with kings by him was seen;

The same who with the seven heads was born,
And power and strength from the ten horns received,
So long as virtue to her spouse was pleasing.

Ye have made yourselves a god of gold and silver;
And from the **idolater** how differ ye,
Save that he one, and ye a hundred worship?

Ah, Constantine! of how much ill was mother,
Not thy conversion, but that marriage **dower**
Which the first wealthy Father took from thee!"

And while I sang to him such notes as these,
Either **that** anger or that conscience stung him,
He struggled violently with both his feet....

A manuscript page from Dante's *Divine Comedy* showing Dante and Virgil in Hell, encountering "souls being devoured by their own remorse." *Reproduced by permission of the Corbis Corporation.*

Grievous: Wounding.

Avarice: Greed.

Afflicts: Causes suffering to.

Depraved: Wicked or sinful.

Idolater: Someone who worships a statue of a god.

Dower: Dowry, or the wealth a bride brings to a marriage.

That: Because.

What happened next ...

Dante was not the only person angered by simony, or by the removal of the papal seat from Rome to Avignon. The Italian poet Petrarch (PEE-trark; 1304–1374), one of Dante's many admirers, called the Avignon papacy the "Babylonian Captivity," referring to the period in the Old Testament when the people of Israel were carried off to slavery in Babylon. Worse was to follow, as the Church became embroiled in the Great Schism (SKIZ-um; 1378–1417). During the Great Schism, there were not two but *three* rival popes: one in Rome, one in Avignon, and one in the Italian city of Pisa.

Infighting among Catholics weakened the Church, and made it vulnerable to the early stirrings of the Reformation (ref-ur-MAY-shun), an effort to reform the Christian religion. One of the most prominent leaders of the Reformation was the German preacher Martin Luther (1483–1546), who became outraged at a practice not unlike simony: the sale of indulgences, whereby popes and priests were charging believers money in exchange for forgiveness from God. Like Dante's work, the Reformation—which gained strength because of corruption in the Catholic Church—helped pave the way for massive changes in European life at the end of the Middle Ages and beginning of the Renaissance.

Did you know ...

- The term *simony* refers to the magician Simon Magus, mentioned in the New Testament Book of Acts. Simon tried to pay the apostles Peter and John in order to gain the Holy Spirit's power to heal the sick and the lame, and Peter cursed him for behaving as though holy powers could be bought and sold.

- The nineteenth-century poet and painter Dante Gabriel Rossetti (1828–1882)—who was actually born with the name Dante—modeled much of his work after that of Dante Alighieri.

- One of the most famous quotes from the *Divine Comedy* is the phrase that appeared on the gates of Hell, sometimes translated as "Abandon all hope, ye who enter here."

Dante

By writing primarily in Italian, Dante Alighieri—usually referred to simply as Dante—helped usher in an era of increased literary activity throughout Western Europe. After Dante, writers were much more likely to compose in their native languages, rather than in Latin. The latter had remained the language of educated men throughout the Middle Ages, despite the fact that there was no longer an active community of Latin-speakers. Thus it was a "dead language," and Dante's use of Italian brought a refreshing new energy to literature, which in turn helped lay the groundwork for the period of renewed interest in learning known as the Renaissance (RIN-uh-sahnts; c. 1300–c. 1600).

Dante grew up in the city of Florence, which would become home to a number of influential writers and painters. After studying at several great universities, he became involved in complex political struggles that consumed Italy for many years. When in 1302 a rival group triumphed, he was exiled from (forced to leave) Florence with his wife Gemma Donati, who he had married in 1297. He would spend the remaining twenty-nine years of his life in a variety of cities throughout Italy.

In 1293, Dante had completed his first great work, La vita nuova (VEE-tuh NWOH-vuh; "New Life"), a collection of love poems to a woman he barely knew. This was Beatrice Portinari (1266–1290), whom Dante had first met at the age of eight. He had loved her from that time, though perhaps "admired" is a better word: Dante and Beatrice were never lovers, nor was Dante's affection for her that of a lover. Rather, he saw her as a sort of guiding spirit, an image of purity who inspired his work.

La vita nuova honored Beatrice after her death, and later she would figure in one of the world's greatest literary masterpieces: the Divine Comedy, which Dante began writing in 1308 and completed just before his death in 1321. He also wrote a number of other works, including poetry and nonfiction.

For More Information

Books

Dante Alighieri. *The Divine Comedy of Dante Alighieri.* Translated by Henry Wadsworth Longfellow. Boston: Houghton, Mifflin and Company, 1906.

Halliwell, Sarah, editor. *The Renaissance: Artists and Writers.* Austin, TX: Raintree Steck-Vaughn, 1998.

Web Sites

Dante Alighieri on the Web. [Online] Available http://www.geocities.com/Athens/9039/main.htm (last accessed July 28, 2000).

Digital Dante. [Online] Available http://www.ilt.columbia.edu/projects/dante/ (last accessed July 28, 2000).

The World of Dante. [Online] Available http://www.iath.virginia.edu/dante/ (last accessed July 28, 2000).

History and Fiction

4

Historians of the medieval period had quite different standards for evaluating truth and falsehood than do historical writers today. In the modern world, scholars attempt to approach historical information scientifically, sifting through the raw materials of history—that is, the records kept by people of another time—and attempting to form a picture of that era. Of course a modern historian's picture is colored by his or her unique perspective, but at least modern writers of history generally agree that as much as possible, they should set aside their own views and seek the truth from facts.

In the Middle Ages, however, historical writers lacked such standards. They were more apt, for instance, to attribute events to the work of God or gods rather than to conditions such as weather or economics, whose causes and effects can be more clearly understood. Furthermore, it was not at all unusual for a historian to report something that he (virtually all medieval historians of any culture were men) had heard, without making much of an effort to find out whether it was true or not.

Certainly medieval historians were not entirely to blame for this approach. There were no computers for conducting research, and indeed books themselves were hard to come by: in the days before the printing press, books had to be painstakingly written out by hand, and they were closely guarded like the treasures they were. Nor was it easy for a historian to travel and conduct interviews. Furthermore, historians, like everyone else, are a product of their times, and tend to accept the prevailing views. In the Middle Ages, people in general were much more likely to seek spiritual answers to questions than to look for scientific explanations, and few historians thought differently.

These facts, however, do not fully explain the approach taken by **Procopius** (proh-KOH-pee-us; died c. 565) in his *Secret History*. A citizen of the Byzantine (BIZ-un-teen) Empire, which grew out of the Eastern Roman Empire in Greece, Procopius lived during the reign of the emperor Justinian (ruled 527–65). Many historians today regard Justinian as perhaps the greatest of Byzantine rulers, but one would not know it from the *Secret History*, which portrays him as a murderer and a thief. Even worse was Procopius's depiction of the empress Theodora (c. 500–548), Justinian's wife, whose sex life he described in terms that would make many a modern reader blush.

On the one hand, the *Secret History* is a genuine historical work; on the other hand, it is more like the tabloid newspapers of today that cover the deeds and misdeeds of Hollywood stars. Procopius had written other, more respectable, historical works, but in the *Secret History* he seemed to be saying what he really thought of the empire's royal couple. This bad feeling resulted from deep-seated political differences, but Procopius made little effort to hold his views in check. However, when he wrote that Justinian and Theodora were fiends (demons) in human form, he was not—by the standards of his time—making an outlandish claim. From the perspective of the Middle Ages, demons were a part of everyday life, and it was not farfetched to believe that one could assume the form of an emperor.

The role of magic and the supernatural was no less prominent in East Asia than in Europe, as an excerpt from *Romance of the Three Kingdoms* by **Lo Kuan-chung** (GWAHN-zhoong; c. 1330–c. 1400) illustrates. Describing events that took place more than a thousand years before, Lo Kuan-chung portrayed a period of great upheaval in Chinese history, when the country was torn apart by war. Yet in his version, the Three Kingdoms period of the A.D. 200s became a highly romantic, adventurous time.

Romance of the Three Kingdoms is of great value to historians, but it is not really historical writing: rather, it is a novel, an extended work of fiction. Thus although his book fell into the category known as historical fiction, Lo Kuan-chung was not subject to the same sort of restrictions that govern (or should govern) the work of true historians. He was free to take liberty with the truth if it suited him, and readers of his book did not have to worry that he would allow the facts to interfere with a good story.

William of Malmesbury (MAWMS-bur-ee; c. 1090–c. 1143), in contrast to both Procopius and Lo Kuan-chung, was doing work similar to that of a modern historian. In an excerpt from *Gesta regum Anglorum,* his chronicle of England's kings, he discusses the Norman Conquest of England in 1066, when invaders led by William the Conqueror (c. 1028–1087) from Normandy in France seized the English throne.

This event was one of the most important in the history of the English-speaking world, and Malmesbury wrote about the subject with the kind of serious, thoughtful approach that it deserved. Instead of blaming supernatural forces, or other causes that could not be explained, he looked for an explanation of the Norman victory in the events that preceded the invasion. Not only had the defenders of England been ill-prepared for their actual battle with the Normans, he indicated, but in fact all of England had grown soft from years of excessive luxury. Other historians might disagree with this analysis, but at least it was an idea that could be argued, rather than being a mere matter of belief that could not be disproved.

Procopius

Excerpt from Secret History
Published in *Secret History*, 1927

The writings of the Greek historian Procopius (proh-KOH-pee-us; died c. 565), including *History in Eight Books* and *On Buildings,* have certainly inspired much admiration from scholars of the medieval world. Yet these works, respectable as they are, are not nearly as entertaining—nor do they receive as much attention today—as a gossipy, scandalous book called *Secret History,* which Procopius never intended to publish. Chock-full of tall tales, and so slanted with the writer's own opinions that it barely qualifies as a serious historical work, *Secret History* is nonetheless more intriguing than the hottest soap opera on television.

In Procopius's time, the Byzantine (BIZ-un-teen) Empire, which grew out of the Eastern Roman Empire in Greece, was ruled by the emperor Justinian (483–565; ruled 527–565). Justinian, often considered the greatest Byzantine emperor, set out to reconquer lands that had once belonged to the Western Roman Empire, and in this undertaking he relied on his brilliant general Belisarius (c. 505–565). Procopius, who served as Belisarius's advisor, wrote an account of these wars in his *History in Eight Books,* which presented Justinian and

"To me, and many others of us, these two seemed not to be human beings, but veritable demons, and what the poets call vampires: who laid their heads together to see how they could most easily and quickly destroy the race and deeds of men."

Procopius

One of the most noted historians of the Byzantine Empire, Procopius came from the region of Caesarea (se-suh-REE-uh) in what is now Israel. He spent his early career as advisor to one of the empire's greatest generals, Belisarius (bel-i-SAHR-ee-us; c. 505–565), serving alongside him in a series of military expeditions from 527 to 531, and again from 536 to 540. During this time, the Byzantines waged war with the Persians in what is now Iran; with the Goths in Italy; and with the Vandals—who, like the Goths, were a barbarian tribe that had helped bring down the Western Roman Empire—in North Africa.

Out of this experience came *History in Eight Books,* a highly acclaimed book. In it, he lavished praise on Justinian (ruled 527–65), the emperor who had ordered Belisarius's conquests. He also wrote *On Buildings,* a six-volume work concerning buildings erected under the reign of Justinian—and again, the book was full of nothing but kind words for the man whom historians consider the greatest of Byzantine emperors.

Privately, however, Procopius held deep grudges against Justinian, Justinian's wife Theodora (c. 500–548), and others in the imperial court. These grudges found expression in *Secret History,* which, as its name implies, was something Procopius wrote without the intention of ever publishing it. Indeed, it was not published until centuries after his death; if it had appeared in Procopius's own lifetime, Justinian would certainly have had Procopius imprisoned or even executed for writing it.

Belisarius as great leaders. Their portrayal in *Secret History,* however, was quite different.

Secret History depicts Belisarius as a fool whose wife cheated on him constantly; as for Justinian, Procopius made him out to be a sort of gangster who helped himself to other people's wealth and killed anyone who got in his way. Even worse was Procopius's depiction of Justinian's wife, Theodora (c. 500–548), who he portrayed as a lustful, scheming woman. Chapter titles from *Secret History* say it all: "How Justinian Killed a Trillion People"; "How Justinian Created a New Law Permitting Him to Marry a Courtesan" (or prostitute—referring to Theodora); and the title of the chapter from which the following excerpt is drawn, "Proving That Justinian and Theodora Were Actually Fiends [demons] in Human Form."

Things to remember while reading the excerpt from *Secret History*

- Procopius intended his *Secret History*—published centuries after his death—only for close friends who shared his views; had the book seen the light of day during Procopius's lifetime, Justinian would certainly have had its author imprisoned or executed. As it is, the book is damaging to Procopius's enduring reputation as a serious historian, since his observations were motivated not by a quest for truth, but by personal grudges.

- The roots of Procopius's conflict with the emperor and empress lay in a larger struggle between two groups that dominated Byzantine life, the Greens and the Blues, named for the colors of their respective horse-racing teams. The specific political differences between the two groups hardly matter in the context of the *Secret History:* what matters is that Procopius was a Green, and Theodora supported the Blues. As emperor, Justinian had to appear to be above the Blue-Green conflict, but it is easy to guess that his sympathies lay with his wife.

- Procopius's claim that Justinian and Theodora were actually demons in human form was not as far-fetched—from the perspective of his time and place, that is—as it might seem. To the medieval mind, supernatural forces were as real and ever-present as the Sun and Moon; therefore it would not have seemed at all unbelievable to Procopius's readers, for instance, that Justinian's father was a demon, who left "evidence of his presence perceptibly where man consorts with woman." (In other words, the demon left some sort of physical evidence that he had engaged in sexual intercourse with Justinian's mother.)

Emperor Justinian. In spite of Procopius's low opinion of him, Justinian is regarded by many historians as the greatest ruler of the Byzantine Empire.
Reproduced by permission of the Library of Congress.

- The emperor Justin (ruled 518–27) was Justinian's uncle, under whom Justinian served as an administrator. As for Hecebolus (hek-EB-uh-lus), he was one of Theodora's lovers from her days as an actress. When he became governor of a Byzantine province, Procopius reported in another chapter of the *Secret History,* Theodora followed him there, but later Hecebolus left her with no money.

Excerpt from Secret History

*... [T]o me, and many others of us, these two [Justinian and Theodora] seemed not to be human beings, but **veritable** demons, and what the poets call vampires: who laid their heads together to see how they could most easily and quickly destroy the race and deeds of men; and assuming human bodies, became **man-demons,** and so **convulsed** the world. And one could find evidence of this in many things, but especially in the superhuman power with which they worked their will.*

*For when one examines closely, there is a clear difference between what is human and what is **supernatural.** There have been many enough men, during the whole course of history, who by chance or by nature have inspired great fear, ruining cities or countries or whatever else fell into their power; but to destroy all men and bring **calamity** on the whole inhabited earth remained for these two to accomplish, whom **Fate** aided in their schemes of corrupting all mankind. For by earthquakes, **pestilences,** and floods of river waters at this time came further ruin, as I shall presently show. Thus not by human, but by some other kind of power they accomplished their dreadful designs.*

*And they say his mother said to some of her intimates once that not of Sabbatius her husband, nor of any man was Justinian a son. For when she was about to conceive, there visited a demon, invisible but giving evidence of his presence **perceptibly** where man **consorts** with woman, after which he vanished utterly as in a dream.*

*And some of those who have been with Justinian at the palace late at night, men who were pure of spirit, have thought they saw a strange **demoniac** form taking his place. One man said that the*

Veritable: True.

Man-demons: Demons in human form.

Convulsed: Troubled or disrupted.

Supernatural: Something beyond the natural world; can refer either to God and angels, or to the devil and demons.

Calamity: Destruction.

Fate: Destiny. Greek writers often viewed Fate as an actual force with a personality; hence the capitalization.

Pestilences: Diseases.

Perceptibly: Visibly.

Consorts (v.): Associates.

Demoniac: One possessed by a demon.

Emperor suddenly rose from his throne and walked about, and indeed he was never **wont** to remain sitting for long, and immediately Justinian's head vanished, while the rest of his body seemed to **ebb and flow; whereat** the **beholder** stood **aghast** and fearful, wondering if his eyes were deceiving him. But presently he perceived the vanished head filling out and joining the body again as strangely as it had left it.

Another said he stood beside the Emperor as he sat, and of a sudden the face changed into a shapeless mass of flesh, with neither eyebrows nor eyes in their proper places, nor any other distinguishing feature; and after a time the natural appearance of his **countenance** returned. I write these instances not as one who saw them myself, but heard them from men who were positive they had seen these strange occurrences at the time.

They also say that a certain **monk**, very dear to God, at the **instance** of those who dwelt with him in the desert went to Constantinople to beg for mercy to his neighbors who had been outraged beyond endurance. And when he arrived there, he **forthwith** secured an **audience** with the Emperor; but just as he was about to enter his **apartment,** he stopped short as his feet were on the threshold, and suddenly stepped backward. Whereupon the **eunuch** escorting him, and others who were present, **importuned** him to go ahead. But he answered not a word; and like a man who has had a **stroke** staggered back to his lodging. And when some followed to ask why he acted thus, they say he distinctly declared he saw the King of the Devils sitting on the throne in the palace, and he did not care to meet or ask any favor of him.

Indeed, how was this man likely to be anything but an evil spirit, who never knew honest **satiety** of drink or food or sleep, but only tasting at random from the meals that were set before him, roamed the palace at **unseemly** hours of the night, and was possessed by the **quenchless** lust of a demon?

Furthermore some of Theodora's lovers, while she was on the stage, say that at night a demon would sometimes descend upon them and drive them from the room, so that it might spend the night with her. And there was a certain dancer named Macedonia, who belonged to the Blue party in Antioch, who came to possess much influence. For she used to write letters to Justinian while Justin was still Emperor, and so **made away with** whatever notable men in the East she had a grudge against, and had their property confiscated.

Wont: Inclined.

Ebb and flow: In this context, "appear and disappear."

Whereat: At which point.

Beholder: Someone seeing something.

Aghast: Amazed.

Countenance: Face.

Monk: A religious figure who pursues a life of prayer and meditation.

Instance: Request.

Forthwith: Immediately.

Audience: Meeting.

Apartment: Room or chamber.

Eunuch: A man who has been castrated, thus making him incapable of sex or sexual desire; kings often employed eunuchs on the belief that they could trust them around their wives.

Importuned: Urged.

Stroke: A sudden brain-seizure that renders the victim incapable of movement or speech.

Satiety: Satisfaction.

Unseemly: Inappropriate or improper.

Quenchless: Unsatisfiable.

Made away with: Got rid of.

Justinian and Theodora

One would not know it from Procopius's *Secret History,* but many historians of the Byzantine Empire view Justinian (483–565; ruled 527–565) as its greatest ruler. Justinian laid the foundations for modern law with his legal code, or system of laws, completed in 535; and under his rule, Byzantine arts flourished.

Even Procopius had to admit that Justinian built a number of great structures, none more notable than the church known as the Hagia (HAH-jah) Sophia. An architectural achievement as impressive today as it was some 1,500 years ago, the Hagia Sophia dominates the skyline of Istanbul, Turkey, which in medieval times was the Byzantine capital of Constantinople (kahn-stan-ti-NOH-pul). Also during Justinian's time, the Byzantine art of mosaics (moh-ZAY-iks)—colored bits of glass or tile arranged to form a picture—reached a high point. The most famous Byzantine mosaics are those depicting Justinian and his wife Theodora, which can be found in Italy's Church of San Vitale.

The Byzantine presence in Italy was an outgrowth of the most visible, yet least enduring, achievement of Justinian's era. Hoping to reclaim the Western Roman Empire, which had fallen to invading tribes in 476, Justinian sent his general Belisarius (c. 500–565) on three military campaigns that won back North Africa in 534, Italy in 540, and southern Spain in 550. These were

Cast down: Depressed.

The leader of a chorus of coins: In other words, wealthy.

Share the couch of: Engage in marital relations with.

Contrive: Plan.

Mistress: Female head of a household.

*This Macedonia, they say, greeted Theodora at the time of her arrival from Egypt and Libya; and when she saw her badly worried and **cast down** at the ill treatment she had received from Hecebolus and at the loss of her money during this adventure, she tried to encourage Theodora by reminding her of the laws of chance, by which she was likely again to be **the leader of a chorus of coins**. Then, they say, Theodora used to relate how on that very night a dream came to her, bidding her take no thought of money, for when she should come to Constantinople, she should **share the couch of** the King of the Devils, and that she should **contrive** to become his wedded wife and thereafter be the **mistress** of all the money in the world. And that this is what happened is the opinion of most people.*

costly victories, however, and except for a few parts of Sicily and southern Italy, the Byzantines did not hold on to their conquests past Justinian's lifetime.

As for Theodora (c. 500–548), she had been an actress before she married Justinian—and in those days, actresses were looked upon as little better than prostitutes, and in fact many actresses were prostitutes. It is doubtful, however, that her morals were nearly as loose as Procopius portrays them in his X-rated account from the *Secret History*, "How Theodora, Most Depraved of All Courtesans, Won His Love." In any case, after Theodora married Justinian and became empress, she proved herself a great help to her husband—and a leader in her own right.

When the citizens of Constantinople revolted against Justinian in 532, the emperor was slow to act, and considered fleeing the palace. Theodora, however, stirred him to action when she said, "For my own part, I hold to the old saying that the imperial purple makes the best burial sheet"—in other words, it is better to die defending the throne than to run away. Thus Justinian maintained power, and went on to the many achievements that marked his reign. When Theodora died in 548, Justinian was heartbroken.

What happened next ...

The Byzantine Empire reached a high point under Justinian, but it began to decline within his lifetime. A plague or disease reached the empire in 541, and did not end until the mid-700s, by which time it had killed millions of people. Aside from everything else, this meant that the empire's tax revenues decreased dramatically, leaving it unable to pay for its armies. A number of neighboring peoples revolted, further weakening Byzantine power.

Procopius mentioned a number of places within the Byzantine Empire: Egypt; the neighboring land of Libya; Antioch (AN-tee-ahk), a city on what is now the border between Syria and Turkey; and the desert beyond. All these lands—along with a great portion of what Justinian had won back from barbarian tribes in Europe—would be lost during the

A famous mosaic from the Church of San Vitale showing Theodora and her attendants. *Reproduced by permission of the Corbis Corporation.*

600s. A new and powerful empire was on the rise, with its roots among the Muslims of Arabia.

The Byzantine Empire seemed doomed, but it managed to hold on, driving back the Arabs who attacked Constantinople in 718. Over the centuries that followed, it won back territories in southeastern Europe, though it never regained the lands it had lost in the Middle East. The empire reached a second high point in 1025, but its defeat by the Turks at the Battle of Manzikert in 1071 signaled the beginnings of a long decline that would bring the Byzantine Empire to an end in 1453.

Did you know ...
- Procopius did not give the *Secret History* its title. When it was first published in the 900s, it was called *Anekdota*, meaning unpublished. The present title only appeared in modern times.

- In 1992, novelist Donna Tartt published a best-selling murder mystery about a group of college students majoring in ancient Greek studies. Its title was *The Secret History.*

For More Information

Books

Chrisp, Peter. *The World of the Roman Emperor.* New York: P. Bedrick Books, 1999.

Evans, J. A. S. *Procopius.* New York: Twayne Publishers, 1972.

Nardo, Don. *Rulers of Ancient Rome.* San Diego, CA: Lucent Books, 1999.

Procopius. *Secret History.* Translated by Richard Atwater. Chicago: P. Covici, 1927.

Web Sites

"Medieval Sourcebook: Procopius of Caesarea: *The Secret History.*" *Medieval Sourcebook.* [Online] Available http://www.fordham.edu/halsall/basis/procop-anec.html (last accessed July 28, 2000).

William of Malmesbury

Excerpt from **Gesta regum Anglorum**
Published in *Readings in European History,* **1904**

In 793, a terrifying force swept out of northern Europe: a group of invaders known as Vikings, Northmen, or Norsemen. Whatever their name, they spread death and destruction throughout the continent for the next two centuries. By the late 900s, however, Vikings had settled in various areas, including a region in the north of France. This area, settled in 911, came to be known as Normandy. Like their forefathers the Vikings, the Normans—their name was a version of "Northmen"—were a restless people, eager for conquest. Early in the eleventh century, a new opportunity appeared for them when Emma, daughter of Duke Richard I of Normandy, married Ethelred the Unready (ruled 978–1016), king of England.

Ethelred was a descendant of invaders from Germany who in the 400s had taken Britain from the Celts, who had controlled the island for a thousand years. Unable to defend themselves after soldiers from the declining Roman Empire departed in 410, the Britons (as the British Celts were called) had actually invited the German tribes—known as the Angles, Saxons, and Jutes—to help them defend their island. But the Germans conquered it instead, and as a result the land took their

"This was a fatal day to England, and melancholy havoc was wrought in our dear country during the change of its lords."

William of Malmesbury

Like many scholars of medieval Europe, William of Malmesbury was a monk in the Catholic Church. His name is taken from the town in southern England where he lived most of his life.

Malmesbury's first notable work of history was *Gesta regum Anglorum* (c. 1125), an account of England's kings modeled on the writings of the noted English historian Bede (BEED; c. 672–735). He followed this with *Gesta pontificum Anglorum* (c. 1126), and *Historia novella,* which covered events in England up to 1142.

name. The main part of Britain came to be known as England after the Angles, and to this day people of English descent are known as Anglo-Saxons.

By 1042, when Ethelred's and Emma's son Edward the Confessor became king, the stage was being set for another takeover, this time by the Normans. Edward, who died in 1066, placed a great deal of trust in Norman advisors; meanwhile, more and more settlers came from Normandy to England. After 1053, the most influential figure in Edward's court was his son Harold (c. 1022–1066), who assumed the throne after his father's death. Harold reigned for less than a year: on October 14, 1066, he died in a battle against an invading Norman force, led by a duke named William (c. 1028–1087)—better known as William the Conqueror. The two armies met on a beach near the town of Hastings, and the victory of the Normans would become one of the most important events in the history of the English-speaking world.

Things to remember while reading the excerpt from *Gesta regum Anglorum*

- The following account comes from the historian William of Malmesbury (MAWMS-bur-ee; c. 1090–c. 1143). His *Gesta regum Anglorum*—like most educated Western Europeans of the Middle Ages, Malmesbury wrote in Latin—is a chronicle of the kings of England, written in about 1125. By that time, Henry I, son of William the Conqueror, ruled England, and the authority of the Normans had been firmly established.

- Malmesbury portrayed both William and Harold as great and brave leaders; however, he was also clear that the English were not prepared for the invasion. In Malmesbury's view, they had grown soft while the Normans kept their minds on their objective: victory. Describing the two armies' preparations for battle, Malmesbury noted that the Normans took communion, a Christian celebration commemorating Jesus' Last Supper before his crucifixion. He used this fact to point out that the Normans were preparing for the upcoming battle, while the English wasted their energies partying. Some medieval historians might have claimed that the Normans won because God was on their side; Malmesbury, by contrast, suggested that the Normans won because of their serious attitude. His discussion of the cause-and-effect relations governing the outcome of the battle reveals the mind of a serious historian.

- The *Song of Roland* (roh-LAHND) is a great tale, not so different from the stories of King Arthur, that concerns a battle in Spain that took place in 778. Roland was a fabled knight serving under Charlemagne (SHAHR-luh-main; ruled 768–814), emperor of what is now France and Germany, in his campaign to repel Muslim invaders. The actual conflict with the Muslims was uneventful; but as with the story of King Arthur, based on real events during the time of the German invasion of the 400s, later poets created an inspiring romantic tale out of these occurrences.

Excerpt from Gesta regum Anglorum

*The courageous leaders mutually prepared for battle, each according to his national custom. The English, as we have heard, passed the night without sleep, in drinking and singing, and in the morning proceeded without delay against the enemy. All on foot, armed with battle-axes, and covering themselves in front **by the juncture of their shields**, they formed an impenetrable body which would assuredly have secured their safety that day had not the Normans, by a **feigned flight, induced** them **to open their ranks**, which till that time, according to their custom, had been closely compacted. King Harold himself, on foot, stood with his brothers near the **standard** in order that, so long as all shared equal danger, none could think of retreating. This same standard William sent, after his*

By the juncture of their shields: In other words, by putting their square shields together to form a solid wall—a practice learned from the Romans.

Feigned flight: A pretended retreat or escape.

Induced: Encouraged.

To open their ranks: That is, to go from a tight to a loose military formation, making it easier to attack them.

Standard: A banner soldiers carried into war, which was highly important for its symbolic power.

Infantry: Foot soldiers.

Vanguard: Front or leading edge.

Cavalry: Soldiers on horseback.

Serene countenance: Brave appearance.

Arms: Weapons.

Hauberk: A covering of chain mail, a type of armor.

The hind part before: In other words, backwards.

Ardor: Enthusiasm.

Phalanx: A column of soldiers.

Fly: Flee.

Deceived by a stratagem: Tricked by a clever plan.

Eminence: A hill or high point.

To a man: In other words, they killed them all.

A short passage: A shortcut.

Trod: Trampled.

Hollow: A sunken area.

Melancholy havoc was wrought: In other words, terrible trouble was caused.

Usages: Practices.

Heathens: Godless people.

Rights: Laws.

By degrees: Gradually.

Relegated arms to a secondary place: In other words, made military matters less important.

Clergy: Priests.

victory, to the pope; it was sumptuously embroidered with gold and precious stones, and represented the figure of a man fighting.

On the other hand, the Normans passed the whole night in confessing their sins, and received the communion of the Lord's body in the morning. Their **infantry**, with bows and arrows, formed the **vanguard**, while their **cavalry**, divided into wings, was placed in the rear. The duke [William], with **serene countenance**, declaring aloud that God would favor his as being the righteous side, called for his **arms**; and when, through the haste of his attendants, he had put on his **hauberk the hind part before**, he corrected the mistake with a laugh, saying "The power of my dukedom shall be turned into a kingdom." Then starting the Song of Roland, in order that the warlike example of that hero might stimulate the soldiers, and calling on God for assistance, the battle commenced on both sides, and was fought with great **ardor**, neither side giving ground during the greater part of the day.

Observing this, William gave a signal to his troops, that, feigning flight, they should withdraw from the field. By means of this device the solid **phalanx** of the English opened for the purpose of cutting down the fleeing enemy and thus brought upon itself swift destruction; for the Normans, facing about, attacked them, thus disordered, and compelled them to **fly**. In this manner, **deceived by a stratagem**, they met an honorable death in avenging their enemy; nor indeed were they at all without their own revenge, for, by frequently making a stand, they slaughtered their pursuers in heaps. Getting possession of an **eminence**, they drove back the Normans, who in the heat of pursuit were struggling up the slope, into the valley beneath, where, by hurling their javelins and rolling down stones on them as they stood below, the English easily destroyed them **to a man**. Besides, by **a short passage** with which they were acquainted, they avoided a deep ditch and **trod** underfoot such a multitude of their enemies in that place that the heaps of bodies made the **hollow** level with the plain. This alternating victory, first of one side and then of the other, continued so long as Harold lived to check the retreat; but when he fell, his brain pierced by an arrow, the flight of the English ceased not until night.

... This was a fatal day to England, and **melancholy havoc was wrought** in our dear country during the change of its lords. For it had long adopted the manners of the Angles, which had indeed altered with the times; for in the first years of their arrival they were barbarians in their look and manner, warlike in their **usages**, **heathens** in their **rights**. After embracing the faith of Christ, **by degrees** and, in process of time, in consequence of the peace which they enjoyed, they **relegated arms to a secondary place** and gave their whole attention to religion.

... Nevertheless, the attention to literature and religion had gradually decreased for several years before the arrival of the Normans. The **clergy,** contented with a little confused learning, could scarcely stammer out the words of the **sacraments;** and a person who understood grammar was an object of wonder and astonishment. The monks mocked the rule of their **order** by fine **vestments** and the use of every kind of food. The nobility, given up to **luxury and wantonness,** went not to church in the morning after the manner of Christians, but merely, in a careless manner, heard **matins** and **masses** from a hurrying priest in their **chambers,** amid the **blandishments** of their wives. The **commonalty,** left unprotected, became a prey to the most powerful, who amassed fortunes, either by seizing on their property or by selling their persons into foreign countries; although it is characteristic of this people to be more inclined to **reveling** than to the accumulation of wealth....

Drinking in parties was a universal practice, in which occupation they passed entire nights as well as days. They consumed their whole substance in **mean and despicable houses,** unlike the Normans and French, who live frugally in noble and splendid mansions. **The vices attendant on** drunkenness, which **enervate** the human mind, followed; hence it came about that when they **engaged** William, with more **rashness** and **precipitate** fury than military skill, they doomed themselves and their country to slavery by a single, and [at] that an easy, victory. For nothing is less effective than rashness; and what begins with violence quickly ceases or is repelled.

What happened next ...

The Norman Conquest proved to be an event of enormous significance, with a vast impact on the law, culture, and especially the language of England. The Normans spoke French, and this added a Latin-based influence to the Germanic language of England. Thus today English has at its disposal a huge array of words, many rooted in Latin and others in German.

Sacraments: Special religious ceremonies, such as taking Communion or exchanging wedding vows.

Order: A group of monks.

Vestments: Clothing.

Luxury and wantonness: A life filled with excessive eating, drinking, and other worldly pleasures.

Matins: Morning prayer.

Masses: Catholic church services.

Chambers: Living quarters.

Blandishments: Things that distract a person by their attractiveness.

Commonalty: Common people.

Reveling: Partying.

Mean and despicable houses: In other words, taverns or bars known for drunkenness and the loose practices of the people who went there.

The vices attendant on: In other words, the bad things that went with.

Enervate: Reduce the moral and mental health.

Engaged: Started a conflict with.

Rashness: Hastiness.

Precipitate: Quick or hasty.

King Harold of England is hit during the Battle of Hastings. Historian William of Malmesbury explains that Harold's "brain [was] pierced by an arrow."
Reproduced by permission of Archive Photos, Inc.

In the short run, the invasion led to the crowning of William the Conqueror as William I, king of England. Kings of England after William also held the title "duke of Normandy"; and after 1154, an English king was also count or ruler of Anjou (ahn-ZHOO), a French province. Thus the English kings had their eye on France, just as the Normans had once had their eye on England, and this would lead to a series of conflicts between the English and the French. These ten-

The Norman Conquest and the English Language

English is the world's most widely spoken language, with 800 million speakers at the end of the twentieth century. Yet only 310 million of those people are native English-speakers, a fact that testifies to the broad reach of the language: people all over the world, even in places where English is not the native language, use English to communicate.

There are at least two reasons for this, one of which is the fact that Great Britain established a huge colonial empire during the 1700s and 1800s. This ensured that there would be native English-speakers in lands as far away from England as Australia and New Zealand, India and Pakistan, South Africa—and, of course, the United States.

The other reason behind the wide acceptance of English is its large vocabulary: the language includes more than 600,000 words, along with some 400,000 technical terms. Though the average English-speaker only uses about 60,000 words, it is clear that English offers a wide variety of ways to say things. And if a word does not exist in English, one can simply be borrowed from another language and included in the English vocabulary.

This tradition of borrowing words goes back to the Norman Conquest of 1066. Prior to that time, the Anglo-Saxon inhabitants of Britain spoke what is now known as Old English, a language closely related to German. But the invading Normans brought the French language with them, and this gave English a whole new range of words. Historians date the development of Middle English, with its much richer vocabulary, from the Norman Conquest. Some 400 years later, the invention of the printing press brought about another great expansion in the language, as books and ideas were much more easily distributed; this in turn led to the development of English as it is spoken today.

sions would explode in the Hundred Years' War (1337–1453), and ill-will between Britain and France would continue into the modern era, until British forces defeated the French armies under Napoleon in 1815.

Did you know ...

- During World War II (1939–45), Normandy itself was the site of an invasion by a much larger force than the one the Normans had sent to England nine centuries before.

DVVILGELM VM: NORMANNO RV M: DVCEM

A scene from the Bayeux Tapestry showing an encounter between King Harold of England and William the Conqueror.
Reproduced by permission of the Corbis Corporation.

On "D-Day," June 6, 1944, American, British, and other Allied armies landed on the beaches of Normandy. This invasion of the European continent marked the beginning of the end for Nazi Germany.

• A 231-foot-long scroll called the Bayeux (bah-YOH) Tapestry, created during the Middle Ages, provides a visual record of the Norman Conquest.

• The present royal family of England can trace their ancestry back to William the Conqueror.

For More Information

Books
May, Robin. *William the Conqueror and the Normans.* Illustrations by Gerry Wood. New York: Bookwright Press, 1985.

Robinson, James Harvey, editor. *Readings in European History,* Volume I: *From the Breakup of the Roman Empire to the Protestant Revolt.* Boston: Ginn & Co., 1904.

Severy, Merle, editor. *The Age of Chivalry.* Washington, D.C.: National Geographic Society, 1969.

Web Sites

"HWC, William the Conqueror." [Online] Available http://history.idbsu.edu/westciv/willconq/ (last accessed July 28, 2000).

"Medieval Sourcebook: William of Malmesbury: The Battle of Hastings." *Medieval Sourcebook.* [Online] Available http://www.fordham.edu/halsall/source/1066malmesbury.html (last accessed July 28, 2000).

Lo Kuan-chung

Excerpt from **Romance of the Three Kingdoms**
Published in *San kuo, or Romance of the Three Kingdoms,* 1925

The people of China, particularly during the premodern era, tended to have a unique view of history. For many centuries during ancient times, the Chinese believed that theirs was the only civilization in the world. It is understandable why they thought this, because they had no contact with the cultures of India, far away across high mountains to the south; nor did they know of Greece or Rome. All around them, they saw only barbarians, or uncivilized people, threatening their borders. Therefore to the Chinese, China was the world.

Coupled with this idea was the notion that history—Chinese history, that is, which in the view of the Chinese was world history—ran in cycles of about three or four hundred years. A new dynasty, or ruling house, would establish power, and enjoy many years of peace and stability. But eventually, signs would appear that indicated that the rulers had lost the "Mandate of Heaven," or the favor of the gods. These signs took the form of natural disasters, along with diseases, and together they indicated that an age was about to end. Great misfortunes would follow, until a new dynasty arose that pos-

"As he drew near the throne, a rushing whirlwind arose in the corner of the hall and, lo! from the roof beams floated down a monstrous black serpent that coiled itself up on the very seat of majesty. The Emperor fell in a swoon. Those nearest him hastily raised and bore him to his palace while the courtiers scattered and fled. The serpent disappeared."

Lo Kuan-chung

Lo Kuan-chung was not the only author of *Romance of the Three Kingdoms*. The original text had been written in the period from A.D. 265 to 316 , not long after the events depicted in the book took place. A century after that, another writer revised the great story; but it was Lo—whose name is sometimes rendered as Luo Guanzhong—who wrote the full tale during the early years of China's Ming dynasty (1368–1644).

Another work partially attributed to Lo is *Shui-hu chuan* (SHWEE-hoo CHWAHN), or *Story of the Water Margin*, which like *Romance of the Three Kingdoms* was a tale drawn from Chinese history. It is not clear whether Lo cowrote that book with Shih Nai-an (SHEE NY-ahn), another writer of the era, or simply revised Shih's text.

sessed the Mandate of Heaven—and then the cycle would repeat itself.

Events seemed to prove this idea: for instance, the Han (HAHN) dynasty, the last before the beginning of the medieval period, lasted just over 400 years, from 207 B.C. to A.D. 220. The period that followed, which lasted until the establishment of the Sui (SWEE) dynasty in 589, was a time of civil war and upheaval; yet thanks to a book called *Romance of the Three Kingdoms,* it would also be remembered as an age of great glory and adventure.

Romance of the Three Kingdoms is a novel, or extended work of fiction, based on records kept at the time of the events it depicts. A thousand years later, these stories were compiled and rewritten by Lo Kuan-chung (GWAHN-zhoong; c. 1330–c. 1400) as *Romance of the Three Kingdoms.* The book is equivalent to works more well known in the West, such as the tales of King Arthur and his knights: in the case of such stories, writers took great liberty with historical facts in order to portray events of the past as glorious and romantic.

Things to remember while reading the excerpt from *Romance of the Three Kingdoms*

• The passage that follows, taken from the opening chapter of *Romance of the Three Kingdoms,* concerns events leading up to the revolt of the Yellow Turbans in A.D. 184. The Yellow Turbans were a splinter group who had adopted an extremist version of Taoism (DOW-izm). This philosophy was based on the teachings of Lao-tzu (low-DZÜ; c. 500s B.C.), who held that the key to peace was inner harmony and contact with nature. Taoism did not become established as a religion until the time of Chang Tao-ling (chahng dow-LING), who supposedly lived for 122 years, from c. A.D. 34 to 156.

- Spellings of Chinese names vary, and though in the late twentieth century scholars adopted a new system, historians of premodern China tend to use the old-fashioned spellings. Thus in most historical texts, the name of the emperor Xian (ZHAHN; ruled 189–220) would be shown as Hsien (SHEN); however, this translation uses the new spellings.

- In China, a person's first name is their family name. Thus Zhang Jue (ZHAHNG ZHWAY) may have been a grandson of Chang Tao-ling, whose name would be spelled Zhang Daoling according to the new system. The "Book of Heaven" supposedly given to Zhang Jue by a mysterious hermit (someone who lives separate from other people) was probably the *Tao te Ching* (dow-day-KEENG) or *Way of Virtue,* a Taoist scripture.

- The city of Luoyang (lwoh-YAHNG), in east central China, served as capital to a number of dynasties. As such it contained the imperial palace, which included areas with grand-sounding names such as the Hall of Virtue and the Dragon Chamber. The dragon was a symbol of Chinese emperors. Imperial eras also received impressive names, such as "Radiant Harmony"; however, there was not necessarily a close relationship between the title and the actual character of the period. Thus the era of "Radiant Harmony," the beginning of the end of the later Han dynasty, was anything but radiant or harmonious.

- The following passage contains numerous references to magic and supernatural occurrences. Not only was Zhang Jue a sort of magician—something that had very little to do with the original teachings of Lao-tzu—but Emperor Ling also witnessed the sudden appearance of a serpent in his palace. It is not important whether such things were "real" or not; what is important is that the people believed that they were real. Much the same could be said about the natural disasters depicted, which the Chinese interpreted as a sign from heaven that the Han dynasty was about to fall. Modern people would probably say that the disasters were not a sign, but that they did hasten the dynasty's fall simply by causing problems in the empire;

however, it is important to view these events not through modern and Western eyes, but through the eyes of Lo Kuan-chung's readers.

Excerpt from
Romance of the Three Kingdoms

... Han emperors continued their rule for another two hundred years till the days of Emperor Xian, which were doomed to see the beginning of the empire's division into three parts, known to history as The Three Kingdoms.

*But the descent into misrule hastened in the reigns of the two predecessors of Emperor Xian—Emperors Huan and Ling—who sat in the **Dragon Throne** about the middle of the second century.*

*Emperor Huan paid no heed to the good people of his court, but gave his confidence to the Palace **eunuchs**. He lived and died, leaving the **scepter** to Emperor Ling....*

*It fell upon the day of full moon of the fourth month, the second year, in the era of Established Calm [A.D. 169], that Emperor Ling went **in state** to the Hall of Virtue. As he drew near the throne, a rushing whirlwind arose in the corner of the hall and, lo! from the roof beams floated down a monstrous black serpent that coiled itself up on the very seat of majesty. The Emperor fell in a **swoon**. Those nearest him hastily raised and bore him to his palace while the **courtiers** scattered and fled. The serpent disappeared.*

*But there followed a terrific tempest, thunder, hail, and torrents of rain, lasting till midnight and working **havoc** on all sides. Two years later the earth quaked in Capital Luoyang, while along the coast a huge tidal wave rushed in which, in its **recoil**, swept away all the dwellers by the sea. Another evil **omen** was recorded ten years later, when the reign title was changed to **Radiant** Harmony [A.D. 179]: certain hens suddenly crowed. At the new moon of the sixth month, **a long wreath of murky cloud** wound its way into the Hall of Virtue, while in the following month a rainbow was seen in the Dragon Chamber. Away from the capital, a part of the Five Mountains collapsed, leaving a mighty **rift** in the **flank**.*

Dragon Throne: The Chinese imperial throne.

Eunuchs: Men who have been castrated, thus making them incapable of sex or sexual desire; kings often employed eunuchs on the belief that they could trust them around their wives.

Scepter: A baton that symbolized royal authority.

In state: In full formal dignity; not casually, but officially.

Swoon: Faint.

Courtiers: Attendants of a royal person.

Havoc: Disorder or destruction.

Recoil: The act of pulling back.

Omen: A sign of something, usually bad, in the future.

Radiant: Shining.

A long wreath of murky cloud: A trail of smoke.

Rift: A hole or division.

Flank: Side.

Such were some of various omens. Emperor Ling, greatly moved by these signs of the displeasure of Heaven, issued an **edict** asking his **ministers** for an explanation of the **calamities** and marvels. A court counselor ... replied bluntly: "Falling rainbows and changes of fowls' sexes are brought about by the interference of empresses and eunuchs in state affairs."

The Emperor read this **memorial** with deep sighs....

At this time in the county of Julu was a certain Zhang family.... The eldest Zhang Jue ... was **an unclassed graduate**, who devoted himself to medicine. One day, while culling **simples** in the woods, Zhang Jue met a **venerable** old gentleman with very bright, emerald eyes and fresh complexion, who walked with an oak-wood staff. The old man beckoned Zhang Jue into a cave and there gave him three volumes of the "Book of Heaven."

"This book," said the old gentleman, "is the Way of Peace. With the aid of these volumes, you can convert the world and rescue humankind. But you must be single-minded, or, rest assured, you will greatly suffer."

With a humble **obeisance**, Zhang Jue took the book and asked the name of his **benefactor**.

"I am Saint Hermit of the Southern Land," was the reply, as the old gentleman disappeared in thin air.

Zhang Jue studied the wonderful book eagerly and strove day and night **to reduce its precepts to practice**. Before long, he could summon the winds and command the rain, and he became known as the **Mystic** of the Way of Peace.

In the first month of the first year of Central Stability [A.D. 184], there was a terrible **pestilence** that ran throughout the land, **whereupon** Zhang Jue distributed **charmed remedies** to the afflicted. The godly medicines brought big successes, and soon he gained the title of the Wise and Worthy Master. He began to have a following of **disciples** whom he **initiated into** the mysteries and sent **abroad** throughout all the land. They, like their master, could write charms and recite **formulas**, and their fame increased his following.

Zhang Jue began to organize his disciples. He established thirty-six **circuits**, the larger with ten thousand or more members, the smaller with about half that number. Each circuit had its chief who took the military title of General. They talked wildly of **the death of the blue heaven and the setting up of the golden one**; they said a

Edict: Order.

Ministers: High government officials.

Calamities: Great misfortunes.

Memorial: A written record.

An unclassed graduate: Someone who is not formally educated.

Simples: Plants valued for their healing qualities.

Venerable: Distinguished.

Obeisance: Bow.

Benefactor: Someone who gives something.

To reduce its precepts to practice: To turn its guidelines into a plan of action.

Mystic: Someone who studies spiritual knowledge that is beyond everyday experience.

Pestilence: Disease.

Whereupon: At which point.

Charmed remedies: In other words, magic potions.

Disciples: Followers of a religious leader.

Initiated into: Revealed or explained something formerly secret.

Abroad: In this context, *abroad* means "to different places."

Formulas: Magic spells.

Circuits: Organizations.

The death of the blue heaven and the setting up of the golden one: In other words, the end of one era in Chinese history, and the beginning of another.

*new **cycle** was beginning and would bring universal good fortune to all members; and they persuaded people to chalk the symbols for the first year of the new cycle on the main door of their dwellings.*

*With the growth of the number of his supporters grew also the ambition of Zhang Jue. The Wise and Worthy Master dreamed of empire. One of his **partisans** ... was sent bearing gifts to gain the support of the eunuchs within the Palace. To his brothers Zhang Jue said, "For schemes like ours always the most difficult part is to gain the popular favor. But that is already ours. Such an opportunity must not pass."*

And they began to prepare....

Cycle: Age or era.

Partisans: Supporters.

What happened next ...

Zhang Jue led the revolt of the Yellow Turbans, so named because he and his followers wore headdresses of gold—a color reserved for the Chinese emperor. The revolt broke out in 184, and spread throughout China. In 189 a military leader named Ts'ao Ts'ao (DZOW-dzow; c. 150–230) suppressed the uprising. Ts'ao Ts'ao became the effective ruler of the Han dynasty, and in 220 he established a new dynasty called Wei (WAY).

The years from 221 to 265 became known as the time of the Three Kingdoms. The Wei dynasty ruled in the north, in areas once controlled by the Han dynasty; to the south was the kingdom of Wu, ruled by the Sun dynasty; and to the west was the third kingdom, Shu. This period might be compared to the Civil War in America (1861–65): both events represented painful times in the history of their respective nations, and they would be remembered with a great deal of emotion. In America, novels such as *The Red Badge of Courage* (1895) by Stephen Crane and *Gone with the Wind* (1936) by Margaret Mitchell would keep the Civil War's memory alive, and Mitchell at least—like Lo Kuan-chung before her—portrayed the war as a romantic struggle. Crane and Mitchell, however, were depicting events of the recent past, whereas Lo Kuan-chung was writing about something that had happened a thousand years before his lifetime.

It is understandable why Lo Kuan-chung would have wanted to portray the Three Kingdoms era in glowing terms. Despite the problems caused by the near-constant warfare of the period, the era also saw great advances in Chinese learning and culture. Taoism and Buddhism took hold as new religions in the country; Chinese doctors made significant progress in the study of medicine; and during this time, kites, coal as a means of heat, and encyclopedias all made their first appearance in China. Stability returned in 581, as Yang Chien (YAHNG jee-AHN; ruled 581–604) seized the throne in one of the many small states that controlled China during the period; after eight years spent consolidating his power, he took the imperial throne and founded the Sui dynasty.

Did you know ...

- The American writer Pearl Buck (1892–1973), who lived in China for many years, translated the *Romance of the Three Kingdoms* as *All Men Are Brothers* (1933). She also translated *Story of the Water Margin*.

- Mao Zedong (MOW zhay-DAWNG, 1893–1976), China's most important leader during the twentieth century, was an avid reader of medieval Chinese romances during his boyhood. Among his favorite books were *Romance of the Three Kingdoms* and *Story of the Water Margin*.

For More Information

Books

Lo Kuan-chung. *San kuo, or Romance of the Three Kingdoms*. Translated by C. H. Brewitt-Taylor. Shanghai: Kelly & Walsh, 1925.

Schafer, Edward H. *Ancient China*. New York: Time-Life Books, 1967.

Web Sites

Bu-Ching's Three Kingdoms. [Online] Available http://www.geocities.com/ Tokyo/Garden/2744/StartFrame.html (last accessed July 28, 2000).

"Romance of the Three Kingdoms Home Page." [Online] Available http://w3.one.net/~linch9/rtk_idx.htm (last accessed July 28, 2000).

ThreeKingdoms.com [Online] Available http://www.geocities.com/Hollywood/Academy/8100/index.htm (last accessed July 28, 2000).

Index

Bold type indicates main
entries and their page
numbers. Illustrations are
marked by (ill).

DATE DUE